BY ELIOT WEINBERGER

AUTHOR

Works on Paper (1986)
19 Ways of Looking at Wang Wei (1987)
Outside Stories (1992)
Written Reaction (1996)
Karmic Traces (2000)
9/12 (2003)
What Happened Here: Bush Chronicles (2005)

EDITOR

Montemora (1975–1982)
Una antología de la poesía norteamericana desde 1950 (1992)
American Poetry Since 1950: Innovators & Outsiders (1993)
Sulfur 33: Into the Past (1993)
The New Directions Anthology of Classical Chinese Poetry (2003)

EDITOR / TRANSLATOR

Octavio Paz, *Eagle or Sun?* (1970; 1976)
Octavio Paz, *A Draft of Shadows* (1980)
Homero Aridjis, *Exaltation of Light* (1981)
Octavio Paz, *Selected Poems* (1984)
Jorge Luis Borges, *Seven Nights* (1984)
Octavio Paz, *Collected Poems 1957–1987* (1987)
Vicente Huidobro, *Altazor* (1988; 2003)
Octavio Paz, *A Tree Within* (1988)
Octavio Paz, *Sunstone* (1991)
Cecilia Vicuña, *Unravelling Words and the Weaving of Water* (1992)
Xavier Villaurrutia, *Nostalgia for Death* (1992)
Octavio Paz, *In Light of India* (1997)
Octavio Paz, *A Tale of Two Gardens* (1997)
Octavio Paz, *An Erotic Beyond: Sade* (1998)
Jorge Luis Borges, *Selected Non-Fictions* (1999)
Bei Dao, *Unlock* (2000)
Octavio & Marie-José Paz, *Figures & Figurations* (2002)

WHAT
HAPPENED
HERE

BUSH CHRONICLES

BY

ELIOT
WEINBERGER

A NEW DIRECTIONS
PAPERBOOK ORIGINAL

Book design by Sylvia Frezzolini Severance
Cover design by Semadar Megged
New Directions Books are printed on acid-free paper.
First published as New Directions Paperbook 1020 in 2005
Published simultaneously in Canada by Penguin Books Canada Limited

Library of Congress Cataloging-in-Publication Data

Weinberger, Eliot.
    What happened here : Bush chronicles / by Eliot Weinberger.
        p. cm.
    ISBN 0-8112-1638-1 (alk. paper)
    1. United States—Politics and government—2001–
    2. Bush, George W. (George Walker), 1946-
    3. War on Terrorism, 2001–
    4. United States—Foreign relations—2001– I. Title.
        E902.W455 2004
        973.931—dc22

                                        2005015035

New Directions Books are published for James Laughlin
by New Directions Publishing Corporation,
80 Eighth Avenue, New York, NY 10011

CONTENTS

for N.S., A.D. & S.

PRELUDE: THE CITY OF PEACE

[25 January 1991 — Gulf War I]

When they seized power in the year 750, the House of Abbasid, descendants of the Prophet's uncle, acquired an empire of distant reach from India to the Atlantic coast of Europe. Twelve years later, on a day fixed by a Persian astrologer for the prominence of Jupiter, work began on their new capital, Madinat as-Salam, the City of Peace. As center of the empire and image of the world, the city was built in the form of a circle divided by a cross; its four gates the four directions to the four corners of the earth.

For five hundred years, though the edges of the empire eroded and broke off, the city—still known by the name of the village it had replaced, Baghdad—luxuriated. The most cosmopolitan city in the world of that time, with ships docked—there at the confluence of the Euphrates and Tigris—from China, India, Russia, Spain, the North and Black African kingdoms; with its schools of painting, poetry, philosophy, astronomy, philology, mathematics; its translations of the Greek texts that would ultimately impel the European Renaissance; where fortunes could be quickly made and even more quickly spent. (Sinbad, for one, became a sailor because he had dissipated an enormous inheritance on evening entertainment and "costly robes.") Perennial symbol of the metropolis as pleasure palace: I write from a city once known, not so long ago, as Baghdad on the Hudson.

The poets of that city—particularly in its first three hundred years—were noted for their rejection of traditional verse forms, their unembarrassed hedonism in many varieties, their scorn for religious and social orthodoxies, their sycophancy in court and their bitter polemics outside it, their elaborate prosodic techniques and increasingly pedantic literary criticism. Their form of choice was the *qit'a*, literally a "fragment"—not so much a modernist shard from a vanished whole as an arrow of light in the gloom, a twinge of perfection, as in the famous couplet (an entire poem) by the 8th-century poet Abbas Ibn al-Ahnaf:

> When she walks with her girl servants
> Her beauty is a moon between swaying lanterns*

The misanthropic, anti-clerical, skeptical, metaphysical, blind anchorite poet Abu al-Ala al-Ma'arri (973-1052) is generally considered to be their greatest. Among his works is a parody of the Qu'ran, for which he was criticized, but not condemned. It is said that Dante read him in translation, and one could easily mistake the couplet that closes this poem by Ma'arri as yet one more eerie and exact image from the *Commedia*:

> Each sunset warns quiet men who look ahead
> That light will end; and each day postman Death
>
> Knocks on our door. Although he does not speak,
> He hands us a standing invitation.
>
> Be like those skeleton horses which scent battle
> And fear to eat. They wait chewing their bridles.

* The translations are by Abdullah al-Udhari and George Wightman, from their *Birds through a Ceiling of Alabaster* (Penguin, 1975)

Ma'arri wrote:

> Some people are like an open grave:
> You give it the thing you love most
> And get nothing in return.

And, a thousand years ago in Baghdad, he wrote a line that, in New York in late January 1991—days filled with fabricated images of the barbarity of the new enemy we were slaughtering—made me, if only for a few hours, turn off the television:

> Don't let your life be governed by what disturbs you.

WHAT
HAPPENED
HERE

UN COUP D'ÉTAT TOUJOURS ABOLIRA LE HASARD

[27 January 2001]

A novelist writes me: "Have you noticed that everyone is saying 'Happy New Year' sarcastically?" In the classified advertisements of the *New York Review of Books*, an academic couple, "in the wake of the national election," seeks employment in any other country. A Washington bank executive, whom I barely know, calls to ask what brand of cigarettes I smoke; she's decided to take up the habit again. Friends I meet on the street are less angry than dazed: marooned on the island of CNN for months, they now realize that no rescue ship is coming. The United States has suffered the first coup d'état in its history.

Although no tanks circled the White House and no blood was shed, the word "coup" is only slightly hyperbolic. An illegality declared legal, a corrupt usurpation of power did indeed take place in the nation that imagines itself the world's beacon of freedom. Let me briefly review the story:

Al Gore received some 540,000 more votes than George W. Bush. Presidential elections, however, are determined by the archaic system of an Electoral College, to which each state sends representatives who vote according to the will of that state's voters, nearly always on a winner-takes-all basis. An 18th-century invention, the College was a last-minute political concession to Southern slave owners when the Constitution was written. Representatives were apportioned according to population; slaves, of course, could not vote, but they were considered to be three-fifths of a human in the calculations, thus increasing the populations of the slave states and the number of their representatives. It was also believed at the time, though this has been forgotten, that an elite of respectable electors would prevent the possibility of an inappropriate candidate being chosen by an unpredictable populace. The Founding Fathers had a limited enthusiasm for democracy.

Last November, as everyone now knows too well, the race was so close that the contest for the Electoral College depended on the votes in the state of Florida. The state is governed by George Bush's brother; its legislature is overwhelmingly Republican; and its Secretary of State, in charge of overseeing the election, was the co-chair of Florida's Bush for President campaign.

The state has long been notorious for payoffs under the palms, for a Southern provinciality without Southern hospitality, and a political demagoguery unsweetened by rhetorical flourishes. Predictably, the state's technicalities of voting varied widely. Wealthy white communities, more likely to vote for Bush, had modern voting machines. Black communities— and Bush nationally received even less black votes than Reagan—had antiquated machines which failed to count tens of thousands of votes. In a bizarre incident, thousands of elderly retired Jews, some of them Holocaust survivors, discovered that, because of a poorly designed ballot, they had mistakenly voted for Pat Buchanan, a minority party candidate who has expressed admiration for Hitler.

When the ballots were counted by the machines, Bush had won by 547 votes out of six million cast. In most American elections, such a small percentage automatically leads to a recount. Because the older machines are so inaccurate—even their inventor stated they fail to count 3–5% of the ballots—these recounts are usually done by hand.

The Republican Secretary of State refused to allow a recount, and the Republican Florida legislature declared the election over. After weeks of maneuvers and reversals, the Gore campaign finally reached the Florida Supreme Court, which ordered a recount to begin. Republicans, in the hysterical surrealism of 24-hour news channels, relentlessly charged that the Democrats were trying to "steal" the election, and that humans could not count votes as "objectively" as machines—though hand counts are the practice in most states, including Bush's own Texas. More sinister, in the style of the Indian Congress Party and the Mexican PRI in the days when they ruled, the Republicans brought in paid demonstrators to disrupt the recount. These were housed at the Hilton Hotel, and the reigning Prince of Las Vegas, Wayne Newton, was flown in to serenade them at a special Thanksgiving dinner. Their demonstrations were so violent that the major potential source of Gore votes, the Miami-Dade County election office, was forced to shut down.

It was apparent to all that Gore would win the recount—according to the *Miami Herald*, a conservative newspaper, by at least 20,000 votes. So the Republicans went to the US Supreme Court. The deadline, under Florida law, for selecting the representatives to the Electoral College was December 12. On December 9—when, after endless legal battles, a system was finally in place to accurately count the votes—the Supreme Court stopped everything while it considered the case, on the bewildering grounds that a recount would cause "irreparable harm" to Bush by casting doubt on his victory. (The irreparable harm to Gore was not a consideration.) The vote was 5 to 4.

Supreme Court justices are appointed for life; seven of the nine had been appointed by Republican presidents. Among them, Sandra Day O'Connor had publicly stated that she was eager to retire, but would not do so if a Democrat were elected President. The wife of Clarence Thomas was already working on the Bush transition team, interviewing prospective employees for the new administration. The son of Anthony Scalia was a partner in the law firm representing Bush before the Court. Furthermore, Gore—never imagining they would decide the election—had promised in the campaign that he would appoint no Justices like the rigidly right-wing Thomas and Scalia; Bush had said they were exactly the kind of Justices he wanted. After all, his Dad had picked them.

At 10 p.m. on December 12th, the Court, in another 5–4 decision, ruled against a recount for three reasons: There were only two hours left until the deadline—thanks to them!— therefore it was too late; the Florida Supreme Court had no jurisdiction over an election in Florida; and the recount was unconstitutional, on the grounds that the various kinds of ballots and ways to count them violated the 14th Amendment of the Constitution, which guarantees "equal protection" for all citizens. Although the political bias and mendacity of these grounds were blatant, Bush was now legally and irrevocably the President.

The decision presented a practical dilemma. Every community in the US votes in a different way, with different ballots and different machines. Claiming that this difference was unconstitutional would clearly open the way to challenges to every future local and national election in the country. So the Court, even more astonishingly, also ruled that this constitutional violation only applied to this one election this one time in Florida.

The heart of the matter was articulated by Justice John Paul Stevens, in his dissenting opinion: "Although we may never know with complete certainty the identity of the winner in this year's presidential election, the identity of the loser is perfectly clear. It is the nation's confidence in this Court as an impartial guardian of the law." Americans, until December 12th, had a blind faith in the Supreme Court: that no matter how corrupt or misguided the Executive or Legislative branches, somehow the lofty disinterest of Justice would prevail. This flagrant politicization of the Court is the greatest shock to the system since Watergate and Nixon's resignation. Its repercussions remain to be seen.

There are coups led by powerful individuals to install themselves, and coups where powerful forces install a figurehead. This American version is clearly the latter. In terms of previous government service, George W. Bush is the least qualified person ever to become President. For most of his life, he has been a type familiar to most of us from late adolescence: the bad boy rich kid, the one who always has a new idea for a party or a prank. Grandson of a well-known Senator and Ambassador; son of a Congressman, Ambassador, CIA chief, Vice President, and President; his family connections got him into Yale and Harvard, where he spent his time on things like personally branding the initiates of his fraternity with a hot iron. Having graduated with the old Ivy League "Gentleman's C," the family secured him loans of millions of dollars from wealthy friends to start a series of businesses that all failed.

Success came when his father was elected President. A group of Texas millionaires decided to buy a mediocre baseball team, and they shrewdly installed the President's son as general manager. His mission was to persuade Texas to build a stadium for the team, entirely at taxpayers' expense. He succeeded, and a luxurious stadium was built, drawing the crowds. There was no doubt that Bush Jr. was a friendly and persuasive guy and, now that he had renounced his lifelong excesses with alcohol and drugs and, as they say, let Jesus Christ into his heart, it was apparent on the golf courses where these decisions are made that Jr. would make a fine governor. A few months after his election, the baseball team was sold for a fortune, and the partners decided to give him many millions more—out of their own pockets—than his proper share. This was, of course, to reward his fine work, and not because he was the Governor with billions of dollars of contracts to award.

Bush may not be as stupid as he is tirelessly portrayed by cartoonists and television comedians—the most popular website of the moment is *bushorchimp.com*, comparative photographs of Bush and chimpanzees—but he may be the least curious person on earth. What is known about him is what he does not do. He does not read books, go to the movies, watch television, or listen to music of any kind. Despite his wealth, his only travels outside of the US have been a single beach vacation in Mexico, a short business trip to Saudi Arabia, and a summer vacation in China when his father was Ambassador, where he spent his time, reportedly, trying to "date Chinese women." During the five weeks when the election results were being contested, Bush remained secluded at his ranch, where he does not have a television. In other words, he was the one person in America not transfixed by the intricacies of the continuing story. Like a Chinese Emperor, his only source of information was what his ministers told him.

He is in bed by ten and takes long naps during the day; he always carries his beloved pillow with him. He likes to play solitaire on a computer and something called Video Golf; his favorite food is a peanut butter sandwich. As Governor, he never read reports, but depended on summaries from assistants; details bore him. His difficulties with the English language are legendary, and there is a website, updated daily, of his mangled sentences. One journalist has speculated that he has a serious reading disability. Bush responded—and this is neither a joke nor apocryphal—"That woman who said I have dyslexia, I never even interviewed her!"

Yet, almost half of the voters (that is, 24% of the eligible voters, since only 50% actually voted) voted for him, thanks less to Bush's abilities than to Gore's ineptness. Gore, in a neurotic insistence on disassociating himself from Clinton as a person—even though no one imagined he'd be having Monicas under his desk—refused to run on the eight Clinton-Gore years of economic prosperity. Nor did he ever bother to link Bush to the more unpopular aspects of the Republican Party, including their continual investigations of Clinton and the impeachment hearings—a six-year, slow-motion coup attempt that ultimately failed. The election, in the end, came down to who was perceived as a nicer guy. Gore had the mannerisms of a very nervous kindergarten teacher trying to be patient, while Bush was simply the guy who brings the beer to the party.

The last friendly dodo to be President, Ronald Reagan, was extreme in his servitude to what Eisenhower famously called the "military-industrial complex." Taxes on corporations and the rich were cut to almost nothing, defense spending escalated astronomically, the country went from a surplus to a trillion-dollar deficit, the middle class became poor, and the poor were devastated. Bush, however, belongs to a new power structure, one that may well prove even more frightening: the military-industrial-Christian fundamentalist complex.

It is clear to everyone, left and right, that the least important man in the new administration is George W. Bush. His ignorance of all aspects of government and the world is so complete that he will be depending entirely on the advice of those in the senior positions. Many of them come from the Pentagon. His Vice President, Dick Cheney—universally seen as potentially the most powerful Vice President ever—was Bush Sr.'s Secretary of Defense during the Persian Gulf War. The Secretary of State, General Colin Powell, is a charismatic man with a moving personal story of rising from poverty, but it should not be forgotten that he helped cover up the My Lai massacre during the Vietnam War, oversaw the *contras* in Nicaragua, and led both the invasion of Panama and the Gulf War. (His appointment is also a violation of the unwritten rule that the State Department and the Pentagon, the diplomats and the generals, should remain separate to keep each other in check.) The Secretary of Defense, Donald Rumsfeld, is an old Cold Warrior who served in the same position under Gerald Ford in the 1970s and presumably has been defrosted from a cryogenic tank. He is well known for his opposition to all forms of arms controls and enthusiasm for warfare conducted in outer space.

Their principal concerns will be to resurrect Reagan's science-fiction Star Wars defense system (against whom is unclear) and, equally terrifying, a return to Iraq. In their circles, the Gulf War is seen as a failure because it did not end with the assassination of Saddam Hussein. Bush must vindicate his father, and Cheney and Powell must vindicate themselves. On Day One of the Bush presidency, the front pages of the newspapers were already carrying stories about the buildup of "weapons of mass destruction" in Iraq. The only spontaneous news, of course, is earthquakes and plane crashes; the rest is always created by someone. If the economy sinks, as it probably will, a return to Iraq will certainly be the most expedient distraction.

Clinton's corporate friends tended to be from Wall Street or Hollywood; his last act as President was to pardon a long list of white-collar swindlers and thieves. But at least his corporate allies were environmentally benign. Bush's capitalist universe is the Texan world of oil, energy, mining, and logging corporations.

Clinton had put a freeze on the economic exploitation of federal lands and declared millions of acres as protected wilderness areas. Bush has already announced his intention to open up those lands, most notably in Alaska, for mining and oil drilling. (Even his loyal brother is fighting him over plans to set up oil derricks off the Florida beaches.) While Bush was Governor of Texas, Houston became the most polluted city in America because he instituted a policy of voluntary compliance with pollution regulations—and, needless to say, none of the heavy industries bothered to comply. His new Secretary of the Interior, Gayle Norton, refused to prosecute polluters when she was Attorney General of Colorado, enthusiastically supports mining and drilling in the national parks and voluntary compliance with environmental laws, does not believe that global warming is caused by humans and, most bizarrely, opposes regulations to prohibit lead in paint. The new head of the Environmental Protection Agency was the Governor of New Jersey, the second most polluted state (after Texas), where she also promoted voluntary compliance. The new Secretary of Labor is anti-union, and opposed to minimum-wage laws and workplace safety regulations. The new Secretary of Energy is a former Senator who unsuccessfully introduced a bill to abolish the Department of Energy.

This is bad enough, but reminiscent of the Reagan-Bush era when, to take one of many examples, the person in charge of the protection of endangered species was a big-game hunter whose office was decorated with the heads of the exotic animals he'd shot. What will be new in the Bush Era is the power of the Christian Right.

During the election, Bush campaigned under the slogan "Compassionate Conservatism." This was generally understood to mean that he was a fiscal conservative with a social heart. Not once did the major media ever examine the meaning of the phrase. It was coined by a certain Marvin Olasky, a former Jewish Communist turned born-again Christian, editor of a fundamentalist weekly magazine, and the author of *Compassionate Conservatism* and *The Tragedy of American Compassion*, as well as such tomes as *Prodigal Press: The Anti-Christian Bias of the Media* and *Telling the Truth: How to Revitalize Christian Journalism*. He is Bush's favorite, shall we say, "thinker," and his vision of compassionate conservatism is a very specific program: Government funds intended to help the poor, the sick, the illiterate, or the drug-addicted should be turned over to private Christian charities. Moreover, not all Christian charities—including some of the best-known—qualify. The only charities to receive these government funds are those where church attendance and classes in Bible study are required for any individuals receiving aid.

Bush attempted such a program in Texas, but was ultimately stopped by the courts. In the first week of his presidency, he has already announced similar plans. As a man who has publicly stated that those who do not believe in Jesus will go to Hell, it is natural for him to ignore the separation of church and state that is one of the foundations of American government.

As a candidate, he tended to keep his fundamentalist connections in the background, and to speak of himself as "a uniter, not a divider." He did, however, happily give a speech at the evangelical college, Bob Jones University, where students are expelled for dating a person of another race, and whose founder called Catholicism "the religion of the Antichrist and a Satanic system."

As soon as he became President, however, he quickly dropped the pretense. His inauguration ceremony was unique in its specific references to Jesus Christ, rather than an ecumenical "God." For Attorney General, the most important domestic position in the cabinet—the one who selects all federal judges and prosecutors, and is responsible for enforcing such things as civil rights, environmental, and antitrust laws—he selected a former Governor and Senator, John Ashcroft, who regularly talks in tongues (as does Justice Clarence Thomas, the only black member of an all-white Pentecostal church) and is a pillar of Bob Jones University. Upon his election as Senator six years ago, Ashcroft poured cooking oil on his head, to anoint himself in the manner of Biblical kings. Last November, however, he was humiliatingly defeated in his reelection bid by a dead man—his opponent had died in a plane crash some weeks before.

Known as the most right-wing member of the Senate—even to the right of the notorious Jesse Helms—Ashcroft has publicly opposed all forms of contraception, the racial desegregation of schools, government support for the arts, pollution regulations, nuclear test-ban treaties, legal protections for women or homosexuals, government assistance to minorities, and even drunk-driving laws. It is said that he believes that the murder of a doctor who performs abortions is justifiable homicide.

Ashcroft is not only opposed to any form of gun control, which might be expected, but he is also connected to an organization called Gunowners of America, which believes that teachers should carry guns as a way of dealing with unruly students. Such views are not extreme around the Bush team, in a country where the leading cause of death among children is gunshot wounds, most of them accidental. As a Congressman, Vice President Cheney voted against a bill that would ban plastic guns, which pass unnoticed through airport metal detectors—a bill that was even supported by the National Rifle Association. A few years ago, after the student massacre at Columbine High School in Colorado, Tom DeLay, a former Texas bug exterminator who is now the most powerful man in Congress, said: "What do you expect, when these kids go to school and are taught that they're descended from a bunch of monkeys?"

Perhaps most bizarre of all, both Ashcroft and Interior Secretary Norton, although born and raised in the North and the West respectively, are obsessed with avenging the defeat of the South in the American Civil War. Ashcroft is associated with a neo-Confederate magazine called *Southern Partisan* that believes that the races were more harmonious under slavery, and that, among many other things, "Negroes, Asians, Orientals, Hispanics, Latins, and Eastern Europeans have no temperament for democracy." The magazine manufactures a t-shirt with a picture of Abraham Lincoln and the words "Sic Semper Tyrannis," which is what John Wilkes Booth shouted when he shot Lincoln. It is the t-shirt Timothy McVeigh was wearing on the day he blew up the government building in Oklahoma City.

Ashcroft is the person who will be responsible for enforcing the laws in the United States. A Supreme Court that has not been so blatantly political since the 19th century will be responsible for the ultimate interpretation of those laws. A smiling rag doll is the President, surrounded by experienced and intelligent military men, industrialists, and Christian fundamentalists who, with a Republican majority in the Congress and no courts to stop them, can essentially do whatever they like. The United States, alas, is not a landlocked nation in the Himalayas or the Andes. Tremors here shake the world.

BUSH SPEAKS

[26 April 2001]

Well, thank you. Thank you, Laura. Once again, thank you all for that warm welcome. I know all of you join me in thanking the authors for being here tonight. The readings were fantastic, and we appreciate it. (Applause.) You've certainly set a high standard for a little reading I intend to do tonight. (Laughter.) Now, some people think my mom took up the cause of literacy—(laughter)—out of a sense of guilt over my own upbringing. (Laughter.) That's one reason why she was so happy I married a teacher. The truth is, I guess I could have paid a little closer attention when I was in English class, but it all worked out okay. (Laughter.) I'm gainfully employed. (Laughter.) And I even have a new book out. And I brought along a copy. Right, here it is. I didn't actually write all of this, but I did inspire it. (Laughter.) Some guy put together a collection of my wit and wisdom. (Laughter.) Or, as he calls it, my "accidental wit and wisdom." It's not exactly *A World Transformed* [by George Bush Sr.], but I'm kind of proud that my words are already in book form. (Laughter.) And I thought tonight I would share a few quotable passages with you. (Laughter.) It's kind of like thoughts of Chairman Mao. (Laughter.) Only with laughs and not in Chinese. (Laughter.) Here's one. And I actually said this. (Laughter.) "I know the human being and fish can coexist peacefully." (Laughter.) Now, that makes you stop and think. (Laughter.) Anyone can give you a coherent sentence, but something like

Transcript of remarks by the President for a "Celebration of Reading," sponsored by the Barbara Bush Foundation; Wortham Theatre Center, Houston, Texas.

this takes you to an entirely new dimension. (Laughter.) Here's another. "I understand small business growth. I was one." (Laughter.) My, do I love great literature. I said this up in New Hampshire. "I appreciate preservation. It's what you've got to do when you run for President." (Laughter.) "You've got to preserve." You know, I really don't have the slightest idea what I was talking about there. (Laughter and applause.) You know, a lot of times on the campaign, they asked me about economics and I actually said this. "More and more of our imports come from overseas." (Laughter.) Now, most people would say this when they're talking about the economy. We ought to make the pie bigger. (Laughter.) However, I said this. (Laughter.) "We ought to make the pie higher." (Laughter.) It is a very complicated economic point I was making then. (Laughter.) But believe me—believe me, what this country needs is taller pie. (Laughter and applause.) And how about this for a foreign policy vision? "When I was coming up, it was a dangerous world. And we knew exactly who the they were." (Laughter.) "It was us versus them." (Laughter.) "And it was clear who the them was." (Laughter.) "Today we're not so sure who the they are"—(laughter)—"but we know they're there." (Laughter and applause.) John Ashcroft, by the way, attributes the way I talk to my religious fervor. In fact, the first time we met, he thought I was talking in tongues. (Laughter.) Then there is my famous statement. "Rarely is the question asked, Is our children learning?" (Laughter.) Let's analyze that sentence for a moment. (Laughter.) If you're a stickler, you probably think the singular verb "is" should have been the plural "are." But if you read it closely, you'll see that I'm using the intransitive plural subjective tense. (Laughter.) And so the word "is" are correct. (Laughter and applause.) Now, ladies and gentlemen, you have to admit, in my sentences, I go where no man has gone before. (Laughter.) But the way I see it is, I am a boon to the English language. I've coined new words, like "misunderestimate"—(laughter)—and "Hispanically." (Laughter.) I've expanded the definition of words, themselves, using "vulcanize" when I meant "polarize"—(laughter)—"Grecians" when I meant "Greeks," "inebriating" when I meant "exhilarating." (Laughter.) And instead of "barriers and tariffs," I said "terriers and barrifs." (Laughter.) We all make our contributions in the world, and I suppose mine will not be to the literary treasures of the western civilization. (Laughter.) But I do hope to contribute in my own way . . .

NEW YORK: THE DAY AFTER

[12 September 2001]

I write in the limbo between the action and the reaction, knowing that the reactions and revelations to come will have already turned these words into a clipping from an old newspaper at the moment they first see print. This, then, is merely the record of a day, some notes from a temporal and emotional limbo.

And it is written from a geographical limbo, for where I live in New York, a mile or so north of the World Trade Center, is not the ruined war zone that is appearing on television, but a kind of quarantine zone. South of Canal Street, the buildings have been evacuated, telephones and electricity are out, and the air is thick with rancid smoke and dust. Between Canal and 14th Street, which includes my neighborhood of Greenwich Village, only residents are allowed to enter—passing through a kind of Checkpoint Charlie, manned by National Guardsmen wearing camouflage suits and carrying rifles, slowly scrutinizing identification cards. There are no cars, no mail, no newspapers; stores are closed; the telephones work erratically. At least the air is clear. The wind is blowing south—everyone has remarked how yesterday and today were among the most beautiful days of the year—while friends downwind in Brooklyn describe their neighborhoods as Pompeiis of ash.

It is, of course, impossible to know what the effects of yesterday's horror will be; whether it will permanently alter the national psyche (if there is one) or merely recede as yet another bundle of images from yet another media spectacle.

This is clearly the first event since the rise of the omnipotence of mass media that is larger than the media, that the media cannot easily absorb and tame. If the media do succeed, national life, beyond the personal tragedies, will continue in its semi-hallucinatory state of continual manufactured imagery. If they fail, something profound may indeed change.

This is the first act of mass violence of this scale to occur in the United States since the Civil War of the 1860s. (Pearl Harbor, to which this has been frequently compared—hyperbolically in terms of consequences, but not unjustly in terms of tragic surprise—was an attack on a military base in an American colony.) We are now experiencing what the rest of the world has known too often. It is the first time Americans have been killed by a "foreign" force in their own country since the Mexican War of the 1840s. (And for Mexicans, of course, the war took place in Mexico.) And it is the first genuine national shock since 1968: the assassinations of Robert Kennedy and Martin Luther King, followed by the riots at the Democratic Convention in Chicago. Despite the incessant attempts by television to fabricate disasters, no one in this country under the age of forty has ever experienced any serious threat to the general complacency.

The personal ramifications are nearly limitless. 50,000 people from all levels of society work in the World Trade Center, and 150,000 visit it daily. Tens of millions throughout the country and the world will personally know (or know someone who knows) someone who died or miraculously escaped, or they will have their own memories of standing on the Observation Deck, looking out on New York harbor and the Statue of Liberty.

In contrast, the second attack site, the Pentagon, is a forbidden zone, as remote as a government building in Oklahoma

City. Had only the Pentagon been hit, there would have been days of hand-wringing over the "blow to our national honor," but it too, like Oklahoma City, would have faded into merely another televised image. The Trade Center, however, is very real to a huge number of people; no sudden crisis, perhaps since the stock market crash of 1929, has so directly affected so many people in this country.

This shock has been compounded by a kind of incredulous despair that, on a national level, there is no one to reassure the citizens and guide them into a future that has become increasingly uncertain. The election (more accurately, the selection) of George W. Bush gravely and perhaps ineradicably undermined confidence in what was the last sacrosanct branch of government, the Supreme Court. Bush's response to yesterday's attacks has now—and perhaps forever—destroyed the last bits of hope that the Presidency would somehow mature him or bring to light some heretofore hidden abilities.

At the news of the attack, he left Florida, where he was visiting an elementary school, flew to a military base in Louisiana, and from there took refuge in the legendary underground bunker of the Strategic Air Command in Nebraska. (A place I haven't heard about since my Cold War childhood: There, we used to be told, the President and government leaders would retreat to keep the Free World free when the atomic bombs fell.) After a day of prevarication, Bush finally showed up in Washington, where he read, quite badly, a five-minute prepared speech, answered no questions from the press, and otherwise had no comments. As always, his face had an expression of utter confusion.

Bush was later followed by the Secretary of Defense, Donald Rumsfeld, whose bizarre press conference, evoking the inevitable Dr. Strangelove, was entirely devoted to security leaks. In a moment of national anxiety, and with hundreds dead in his own department, Rumsfeld devoted his time to complaints that during the Clinton administration people had become lax with classified documents. He grimly warned that sharing classified documents with those who are not authorized to see them could harm the brave men and women of the American armed forces, threatened that anyone sharing classified documents would be prosecuted to the full extent of the law, and urged Pentagon workers to inform superiors if they were aware of anyone sharing classified documents. When asked if the sharing of classified documents had in any way aided the terrorists, Rumsfeld said no and walked away.

No one has yet explained what exactly was on Rumsfeld's mind, but the logic of George Bush's seeming cowardice has received some ingenious explication. Today, administration officials claimed that the terrorist attack was actually an assassination attempt, that the airplane that struck the Pentagon was intended for the White House (but hit the Pentagon by mistake), and that the plane that had crashed in Pennsylvania was somehow supposed to crash into the President's jet, Air Force One. I happened to watch these pronouncements on television with a group of 13-year-olds; they all burst into derisive laughter.

In the postwar period, there have been presidents who have been considered, by the right or the left, as the incarnations of evil (most notably, Nixon and Clinton), but they were seen as evil geniuses. Bush is the first who is universally recognized as a fool. (Even his supporters maintain he's just an ok guy, but surrounded with excellent people.) That in a time of national crisis—a moment when, amidst waning government powers everywhere, government actually matters—the country is being led by a man laughed at by children may create psychic wounds as severe as those caused by the attack itself. It is no wonder that the response deep in America, far from the actual events, has been individualistically survivalist: a huge increase in gun sales, supermarkets emptied of canned goods and bottled water, and long lines at the gas pumps. When there's no government, it's every man for himself.

The perception of Bush's ineptitude has been further heightened by the remarkable performance of New York's Mayor Rudolph Giuliani. I write this with reluctance and amazement, having loathed Giuliani every minute of his eight years as Mayor. He has been an ethnically divisive dictator whose ideology is that, in his own words, "Freedom is authority . . . the willingness of every single human being to cede to lawful authority a great deal of discretion about what you do and how you do it." In this crisis, however, he has become the Mussolini who makes the trains run on time. Unlike his previous self, he has been completely open with the press, with whom he has been meeting every few hours. Unlike every other politician who is filling up television time, he has avoided nationalistic bombast and has limited himself to carefully outlining what the problems are and what solutions he is undertaking. Unlike Bush, he takes all questions, knows most of the answers in detail or explains why he does not. Giuliani's expertise has always been crisis management. His problem as Mayor was that he treated day-to-day government as a continual crisis to be dealt with by a kind of martial law. Now that a real crisis has occurred, he has risen to the task.

The ruling myth in New York City in times of disaster or emergency has always been: "We're all in this together." This is once again the case, which Giuliani has recognized and turned to a general advantage. Unlike the rest of America, New Yorkers have not assuaged their common grief with nationalism and warmongering. They are not buying guns. In the largest Jewish city in the world, they are not attacking the Arabs who run small grocery stores in nearly every neighborhood. (Imagine if this had occurred in Paris or London.) Instead, their response has been an emotional outpouring of support for the rescue workers, firemen, medical workers, construction men, and police. When a convoy of relief teams passes by, people on the sidewalks applaud. So much food has been donated to them that officials are now sending out appeals to stop giving.

New Yorkers—contrary to their image, but not so surprising to anyone who lives here—have responded with a kind of secular *agape*, most evident in the candlelight vigils and makeshift shrines of candles, flowers, and photographs of the missing that are suddenly all over the city. Everyone is out on the streets, subdued and silent in the shock and mourning, but unmistakably there in the need to be around other people. Several times today, friends and even slight acquaintances I have run into—people who know that I don't live dangerously close to the Trade Center and that it would be extremely unlikely that I would have been there—have hugged me and said, "I'm so glad you're alive." It is not a sentiment directed to me as an individual so much as to me as a familiar face, a recognizable part of the community of the living.

I fear that this communal love will not be repeated in America at large, where the prevailing mood is already revenge. (Someone sent me an editorial from a newspaper in South Carolina that warns, "When they hit us with Pearl Harbor, we hit them back with Hiroshima.") If Bush shows any leadership at all, it will be in the name of war. He is surrounded by unrepentant Cold Warriors who, in the days before yesterday, had withdrawn the US from peace treaties and the negotiations between North and South Korea, had encouraged the nuclear buildup of India and (incredibly) China, are obsessed with the comic-book Star Wars defense system, and, perhaps worst of all, had abandoned the Clinton project of disarming the stockpiles of nuclear weapons that remain from the breakup of the Soviet Union. (It is only a miracle that one of those bombs was not on one of those planes yesterday.)

Furthermore, ever since Reagan invaded Grenada—the only "war" since World War II the US actually won—it has become almost predictable that, when the economic news is bad, the President will launch military strikes (Panama, Iraq, Libya) as a domestic diversion and as a way to reverse waning personal popularity. The Bush plan of cutting taxes for the rich, increasing military spending, and sending everyone a check for $300 has turned a huge government surplus which might have been spent on the disastrous American health and education systems into a deficit; the economy at large is a mess. This terrorist attack has occurred in the first recession since Bush Sr. was President, and it is one full of grim forecasts for the future. Bush Jr.'s chances for reelection—the primary motivating force in American politics—have become dim. He needs a war.

And then there is the Curse of the Bushes, which is cowardice. Bush Sr. bailed out of the fighter plane he was piloting in World War II, and the others on board died. Whether or not he was justified, he has been haunted by the charge of cowardice his whole life, and the Gulf War was, in many ways, his attempt to compensate. Even there, in the milieu of macho militarism that he inhabits, he was considered a coward for not "finishing the job" by invading Baghdad and killing Saddam Hussein. Bush Jr., like all of the most militant in the government today, evaded the Vietnam War. He too will feel the need to prove himself a man, and vindicate his father and himself, especially after his initial escape to the SAC bunker.

Worse, Bush will be goaded on by the likes of Condoleezza Rice, one of the most powerful and frightening people in the Bush administration. She is an unlikely, almost unbelievable, incarnation of the Prussian warrior caste ethos as an African-American woman: a body-builder and physical fitness fanatic who keeps a mirror on her desk so she can watch herself speak, an opponent of all forms of gun control, and one who, commenting on relief efforts in Kosovo, said that American Marines were trained to wage war, not deliver powdered milk. In the context of Rice, Rumsfeld, and Vice President Cheney, among so many others, it is terrifying that General Colin Powell of the Gulf War and the My Lai massacre has become the last hope as a voice of reason in this government. He may be the only one who knows that Afghanistan—our most likely initial target—has always been a graveyard for imperial powers, from Alexander the Great to the British to the Russians.

Whether or not yesterday's attack leads to some kind of ground war or politically safer air strikes, and whether or not they in turn lead to further terrorism here, something profound has indeed changed. It is not so much a loss of innocence or security, as a loss of unreality. Since the election of Reagan in 1980, many now refer to the US as the Republic of Entertainment. It's quite true: Less than half of its citizens bother to vote, but nearly all will dutifully line up to buy tickets to whatever blockbuster film has been hysterically promoted. (Films—particularly those this past summer—that no one actually enjoys, with huge box office sales the first weekend and little the following week.) Reagan, as everyone knows, was the master of transforming Washington into Hollywood, with his photo opportunities and careful scripts. Bush has taken this one step further: Whereas Reagan's scenarios were advertisements meant to promote what he was doing, Bush's are often heartwarming television vignettes that are the opposite of his actual policies. Thus we have had Bush in the forest extolling the beauty of the national parks, while opening them up for logging and mining, Bush reading to schoolchildren (as he was yesterday) while cutting the budgets for libraries. Or, my favorite Bush moment: a speech he gave to something called the Boys and Girls Clubs of America, a community-service group, calling them exemplary of what makes America strong and free. The next day, his administration completely eliminated their government funds.

For the last twenty years, Americans have been living in a constant assault of media images, with a continual escalation of sensationalism—much as the Romans had to pour fish emulsion on their food to bring some taste to palates deadened by the lead in their water pipes. Violence has become grotesque, comedies depend on increasingly scatological stupidities which are mistaken for transgressions, adventure films have abandoned narrative to become theme parks offering a special-effects thrill a second, corporations manufacture revolutionary rappers or angry white-boy rock groups, television turns the death of vaguely remembered celebrities into national days of mourning and the forecast of routine storms into dire warnings of potential disaster, and produces an unrelenting stream of Wagnerian tragedies out of the misfortunes of ordinary "real" people.

Of the many indelible images of the Trade Center attack, the one that I think, or hope, will have a permanent effect is that of the plane crashing into the tower. It was immediately perceived by everyone—it couldn't help but be—as a scene from a movie, one that even, by the second day, became available in different camera angles. America, as it has often been said, has become the place where the unreality of the media is the reigning reality, where everyday life is the self-conscious, ironic parody of what is seen on the various screens. But what will it mean when the realization sinks in that this ultimate simulacrum, the greatest special effect ever, led to the very real death of people one knows and the destruction of a place where one once stood?

Perhaps yesterday's attack will sink into collective amnesia, and we will return to the disaster movies and the late-night television comedians who, not surprisingly, are a major source of news for most Americans. For the moment, it is difficult to imagine a return to media fantasy as the opiate of the people. It has been telling that the television news, so accustomed to hyperbole, hasn't a clue how to deal with this story. They have produced it as television: dramatically lit, extreme close-up interviews with the relatives of victims, MTV-style montages set to music, handheld cameras following police and firemen in the manner of "reality" police shows. But unlike everything else that has appeared on television in decades, this story has a personal meaning to millions of its viewers. Despite the best efforts of television itself, this is something that so far has resisted becoming just another television show. Humankind can only bear so much unreality.

Meanwhile, the stories filter in of people I know slightly or well. A man who died in the hijacked plane that crashed into the Pentagon. A man who had a meeting at the Trade Center, but arrived twenty minutes late. A woman who was working on the 82nd floor of Tower 2, saw the plane hit Tower 1, began running down the stairwell, was below the floor where the second plane hit, kept running down the stairs, and emerged unharmed. A photojournalist who had covered the wars in the Balkans and the Middle East, who heard the news, rushed to the scene to take pictures, and vanished. A woman who had stayed home sick. The high school students, two sisters, who had changed trains in the subway station below, ten minutes before, and continued on.

This morning, CNN had a banner that read "MANHATTAN VIRTUALLY DESERTED." My son looked at me and said, "Hey, we're still here!"

NEW YORK: THREE WEEKS AFTER

[2 October 2001]

In the Vietnam War days, there was a kitsch poster, adorned with doves and flowers, that read: "Suppose they gave a war and no one came?" Today's version, less wishful and oddly realistic, might say: "Suppose they declared a war and there was no place to have it?"

America is at war. It has suffered its worst—practically only—domestic civilian casualties since General Sherman burned Atlanta in the Civil War. Most of the country and both political parties have united behind a President who speaks in the language of religious zealots ("crusade"), cowboys ("Wanted: Dead or Alive"), and hunters ("smoke 'em out") to issue non-negotiable demands to foreign governments and openly advocates the overthrow of one of them. Hundreds of ordinary citizens have been arrested on the basis of their names or their appearance, and law enforcement agencies, invoking an emergency, are demanding the repeal of laws that protect civil liberties. Security at all public gathering places has created lines that stretch into waits of hours. Manufacturers of American flags, gas masks, and anti-anthrax medicines cannot meet the demands. Journalists at smaller newspapers have been fired for writing columns that disparaged the President, and some mild criticism from a television comedian was met with a stern rebuke from the White House that, in times such as these, "you should watch what you say." Mosques have been burned; thousands of Arab university students have returned home; hooligans in Arizona murdered a Sikh, though he was neither Arab nor Muslim, for the crime of wearing a turban. And, in a grotesque incident, a car full of white men in Oklahoma shot an American Indian woman, screaming, "Why don't you go back to your own country?"

Here in New York, there has been no violence, and the rage for revenge has been overwhelmed by the mourning for the six thousand or more dead and an outpouring of love for the firemen and other rescue workers, living or dead. The prevailing mood is the listlessness of shell shock, now called post-traumatic stress disorder, compounded by a dread of the future. Chance meetings on the street have the warmth of human contact—we're alive in this together—but on the telephone, people sound abstracted and very far away.

The universal adulation for Mayor Rudolph Giuliani in the first days of the crisis, however, is eroding swiftly, as his original security measures mutate into a kind of martial law. Giuliani must retire on January 1, thanks to the term-limit laws which were passed, with his support, in the 1990s. But, riding the wave of his sudden popularity, and in the unshakable belief in his own indispensability, he has insisted on either repealing the law so he can run again or, at the least, being given an extra three months as Mayor—a violation of the electoral process that is unprecedented in American history. Meanwhile, many days after the initial threat, irrational checkpoints have sprouted up around the city: a potential suicide bomber cannot walk to Wall Street, for example, but he can easily take a subway there. I must show identification whenever I walk down my own street, simply because there is a police station on the next block. (The barricades are manned by suntanned policemen from Florida, who were flown in as auxiliary troops, and who, examining the documents of passers-by, are exhibiting an investigative zeal they notoriously lacked when the hijackers were living in their own state.) Most bizarrely, just a few days ago, Giuliani announced that it was forbidden for anyone, other than accredited members of the news media, to take photographs of the Trade Center rubble or the rescue operations—nearly three weeks after tens of thousands had gone to personally witness the devastation and, not knowing what else to do at such a scene, had taken a snapshot.

America is at war. The climate is one of fear, grief, uncertainty, unity, patriotism, suspicion of neighbors, hatred of the enemy—the war seems to have transformed every particle of ordinary life. And yet there is something missing, and that is war itself.

In the first days following the disaster, certain factions in the Bush administration urged him to immediately bomb Afghanistan, Iraq, Syria, and perhaps Iran, as punishment for harboring or supporting terrorists. A columnist, popular among the Bush crowd, wrote: "We know who the homicidal maniacs are. They are the ones cheering and dancing right now. We should invade their countries, kill their leaders, and convert them to Christianity." Bush himself, who had seemed hesitant and lost in the first few days of the crisis, appeared before Congress a changed and uncharacteristically resolute man. According to the *New York Times*:

> One of the President's close acquaintances outside the White House said Mr. Bush clearly feels he has encountered his reason for being, a conviction informed and shaped by the President's own strain of Christianity. "I think, in his frame, this is what God has asked him to do," the acquaintance said. "It offers him enormous clarity."

There was fear—and there still is fear—that Bush had become the mirror of Osama bin Laden, driven by God to slaughter. It seemed no coincidence that Bush used the word "crusade" for what America was about to do, and that bin Laden's umbrella organization for various terrorist groups was called the International Islamic Front Against Jews and Crusaders. It appeared that a holy war was imminent.

And yet, three weeks later, nothing has happened. No one knows why, but it is assumed that the notorious prudence of Colin Powell—until now, a forgotten man in the Bush cabinet—and possibly some fatherly advice from George Bush Sr. have miraculously prevailed in Bush Jr.'s miasma of inexperience and ignorance. The problem, of course, is that a War on Terrorism is only a metaphor for a war, like the War on Drugs. It is a war with no enemy army and no military targets. The only possible military action would itself be another form of terrorism: bombing civilians in the hope that physical and psychological damage would lead to internal political change. It would be a terrorism, strangely, more in the style of the Algerians or the Irish or the Israelis or the Palestinians in their wars of independence, than of bin Laden, whose theatrical acts of carnage cannot hope to change minds or governments in the West, but which greatly amplify his reputation among certain sectors in the Muslim world.

Bush was quite right, in his address to Congress, when he, in passing, compared terrorists to the Mafia. The US spent most of the 20th century fighting the Mafia—without, happily, carpet-bombing Sicily—and largely without success. (The Mafia dwindled when it started sending its sons to Harvard Business School to learn how to manage the money.) The War on Drugs, thirty years and billions of dollars later, has merely led to a greater proliferation of drugs. Terrorism is a criminal, and not a military, activity, and it is always a scenario of disaster when the military replaces the police.

It is also a mistake to think of Muslim terrorism in strictly political terms. Bin Laden has, of course, stated political goals—withdrawal of the US military from Saudi Arabia, an end to the bombing of Iraq and to US support of Israel—but these are merely ornaments on something much larger. The terrorists are the anti-hero heroes of Radical Islam, and Radical Islam is the Islamic world's form and expression of Youth Culture.

The population has exploded throughout the Muslim world in the last fifty years; in some countries as much as sevenfold. In nearly all Muslim countries, the median age is 18, and a third of the population is between the ages of 15 and 30. These are hundreds of millions of young people with little education, without jobs and without the hope of jobs, packed into expanding and crumbling cities, living in countries ruled by oligarchies, whether secular or religious, of an educated and wealthy elite whose style of life is almost entirely unattainable for the masses. Thanks to television, the young are besieged with images of another world: not only the beautiful movie stars, but the unimaginable luxuries in the living rooms and kitchens of the supposedly ordinary families in comedy shows. Unlike Asia, where there are models nearby of nations that have achieved some semblance of that middle-class glamour, in the Arab world there is only Israel, whose economic success has coincided with the repression of its Muslim inhabitants.

Radical Islam is a classic youth rebellion: total rejection of the values of one's parents; contempt for the dominant culture (which is perceived in stereotypes or abstractions); the invention of an entirely self-contained "alternate lifestyle," with strictly prescribed codes of belief, morals, knowledge, and even dress. Youth movements are fascinated with random and exaggerated violence: the Futurists' demands to burn down the museums; André Breton's description of the true Surrealist as the man who goes out in the street with a pistol and starts shooting; the Yippies' clarion call to go home and kill your parents. These are jokes and not jokes, and they accompany an iconoclastic adulation for those who do indeed commit such violence: the protagonists in bizarre murder cases, or fringe groups of political extremists, like the Weather Underground, the Baader-Meinhof gang, the Red Brigade. In this sense, for the youths of Radical Islam, 2001 is their 1968, and the Trade Center attack a thrilling piece of spectacular political theater far beyond the imaginations of the Situationists. In this sense, the War on Terrorism will only end when this generation becomes middle-aged.

Like all youth movements, it represents a change of consciousness whose concrete manifestations are social rather than political. The Taliban, for example—and the word itself means "student"—much like the youth of the Chinese Cultural Revolution, with their public executions and punishments, have been terrifyingly effective in enforcing mores and customs—the growing of beards, the subjugation of women, the banning of music, television, and all things Western—but they haven't a clue how to feed their own people or rebuild the nation after its decades of war.

The response to youth movements tends to be political or military, and nearly always fails except when there is absolute internal repression (as in Tiananmen Square). In this case, the US government, having created the Taliban monster in its laboratories during the Cold War, is now about to create another monster, the Northern Alliance—a Taliban under another name—as the "freedom fighters" who will liberate the land. It never seems to learn the lesson of what the CIA calls "blowback": the unfortunate consequences of their liberatory intentions. It is a mistake the US has made many times, and it is a mistake to believe that the overthrow of the Taliban will weaken, rather than strengthen, Radical Islam as an international movement.

Meanwhile, three weeks later, we are still marooned in the limbo between the shock of the action and the uncertainty of the reaction. It is the mirror opposite of our continual bombing and starvation of Iraq, where nothing has been said while murderous things have been done. Now everything is said—there is no end to the bombast and threats—but nothing has happened. Hundreds have been arrested, but not a single one has been found who had any conscious connection to the hijacking plot. There is a universal demand for the head of bin Laden, but no evidence has been produced that he was involved, except ideologically. There is a general panic about biological and chemical weapons, but no proof that other terrorist groups either have them or would be able to use them. Troopships and warplanes have been sent to the Middle East and Central Asia, but they remain, as of today, still mercifully idle.

Meanwhile, three weeks later, what has been most moving about the crisis has been a sense of community, of a common humanity, united not only by grief and outrage and love, but by storytelling. New York is the World City. Half of its inhabitants were born in another country, and most of the rest are their children. (A fact apparently not taken into consideration by the hijackers or the intellectuals abroad who have been bizarrely celebrating the hijackers: This blow against the American Empire killed many hundreds who were not

Americans, and the many thousands of the living who are now jobless without benefits are mainly from Third World countries.) Anything that happens anywhere in the world, from a natural disaster to a political campaign, has repercussions here. So naturally an event of this magnitude here has been felt everywhere.

A national shock like the Kennedy assassination essentially led to personal variations of a single story: where I was when I heard the news. But the Trade Center attack has had expanding and tangling ramifications throughout the world. For the last three weeks, I've been spending my days listening to stories, not all of them tragic, and quite unlike the tales of extraordinary self-sacrifice and heroism that fill the newspapers:

The Belgian who celebrated his birthday on September 11 by taking his girlfriend to the seaside. Strolling through the town, they passed an appliance store with a wall of televisions in the window, all showing the jet crashing into the Twin Towers. Assuming it was some disaster movie, they walked on.

The woman whose husband worked on the 80th floor of one of the towers and whose son was on a United flight from Newark to San Francisco. For many hours she did not know if her son had been the unwitting agent of her husband's death, and even worse, her last conversation with her husband had been a bitter argument. But her son had taken a flight that left an hour earlier, and the argument had caused her husband to arrive late for work.

The Indian who reported the rage at Bombay airport, where security forces were confiscating the large and potentially bomb-concealing jars and tins of homemade pickles, a source of family pride that Indians always carry back to their homes abroad or when visiting relatives. The heaps of pickle containers had turned the airport into a warehouse, unusually pungent.

The woman from an internet chat-group of knitters, who told of a member in Australia who wanted to do something, realized that knitting is what she does best, and decided to knit a blanket to send to New York. Sitting on a bus in Adelaide, the passenger in the next seat wondered what she was making, and when it was explained, asked if she also could knit a few rows. Then other passengers asked, and the yarn was passed around. Finally the driver stopped the bus so that he too could work a little on the blanket.

The woman who was on a plane from Chicago to Denver when the Trade Center was hit. She watched the stewardesses suddenly going into the cockpit to speak to the pilots. They emerged weeping, whispering among themselves, then regained their composure and smilingly pushed the beverage cart down the aisle, dispensing drinks, without a word of explanation.

The American who had recently moved to a small village in France, where he had been met with the silent indifference of villagers anywhere. But on the day following the attack, most of the village came by, bringing food and flowers.

And, while the e-mails are full of falsified versions of the inevitable Nostradamus, one friend, who had turned to Herman Melville for a momentary escape, found these eerie words in the first chapter of *Moby-Dick*:

> And, doubtless, my going on this whaling voyage, formed part of the grand programme of Providence that was drawn up a long time ago. It came in as a sort of brief interlude and solo between more extensive performances. I take it that this part of the bill must have run something like this:

"Grand Contested Election for the Presidency of the United States."
"WHALING VOYAGE BY ONE ISHMAEL."
"BLOODY BATTLE IN AFFGHANISTAN."

And another friend, reading Simone de Beauvoir's American diaries, found this entry for January 26, 1947:

> The sun is so beautiful, the waters of the Hudson so green that I take the boat that brings Midwestern tourists to the Statue of Liberty. But I don't get out at the little island that looks like a small fort. I just want to see a view of the Battery as I've often seen it in the movies. I do see it. In the distance, its towers seem fragile. They rest so precisely on their vertical lines that the slightest shudder would knock them down like a house of cards. When the boat draws closer, their foundations seem firmer, but the fall line remains indelibly traced. What a field day a bomber would have!

NEW YORK: FOUR WEEKS AFTER

(SHRAPNEL)

[9 October 2001]

After ordering the bombing of Afghanistan on October 7, George Bush went out on the lawn to play with his dog and practice his golf swings. Since September 11, he has maintained his normal schedule of working until 6 p.m., four days a week, and leaving at noon on Fridays for long weekends at his ranch or the Camp David retreat. Never has an American President in a crisis looked so rested.

Along with the Tomahawk cruise missiles and the bombs falling from F–14s and F–16s, B–52s, B–1s and B–2s, the US also dropped 37,500 "Humanitarian Daily Ration" packets, a single meal—complete with "moist towelettes"—in a country where four million are starving. These packets contained peanut butter and jelly sandwiches. Peanut butter sandwiches are iconic in the Bush family. Bush Jr. has stated that it is his favorite food. Bush Sr., shortly after he was elected President, outlined his vision of the future in these terms: "We need to keep America what a child once called 'the nearest thing to heaven.' And lots of sunshine, places to swim, and peanut butter sandwiches."

The original name of the mission, "Infinite Justice," was changed when Muslim clerics complained that only Allah may dispense infinite justice. The new name, "Enduring Freedom," was meant to proclaim that American freedom endures, but it now means that the Afghans must endure American freedom.

We are bombing Afghanistan in reprisal because it is believed that the terrorists who attacked the Trade Center and the Pentagon were housed and trained for their mission in Afghanistan. There is, as yet, no evidence for this assertion. What has been proven, however, is that the terrorists were housed and trained for their mission in Florida.

We are bombing Afghanistan to overthrow the repressive Taliban regime, which was of little interest to the US government on September 10. To this end, we are supporting the "freedom fighters" of the Northern Alliance, whose rule, from 1992 to 1996, was marked by internecine warfare, shifting alliances, betrayals, and the deaths of tens of thousands of civilians. Or we are supporting—and it would be laughable if it weren't so sad—the restoration of the King of Afghanistan, now 86 years old and never known for any leadership abilities. The Taliban brought an immediate order, however monstrous, to the country: It held public executions for social crimes, but it did not slaughter the masses. In brief: The Taliban is bad and the alternatives are worse.

In order to justify a military build-up and intervention, we have had to turn a small group of criminal outlaws into a full-scale enemy. The actual affinities of the hijackers are unknown, but it may be assumed that they were at least ideologically sympathetic to Osama bin Laden, the leader of one of many terrorist groups. Bin Laden, undoubtedly to his delight, has now been turned into the mastermind of all terrorist groups, tightly connected and organized as the al-Qaeda network, which in turn has been portrayed as part and parcel of a national government, the Taliban, which has, although few, traditional military targets. With the invention of an enemy, the military must naturally exaggerate the capabilities of that enemy, a scenario familiar from the Cold War. The military cannot understand that against our billions of dollars of high-tech weaponry, the "enemy" attacked, and won the battle, with a handful of box-cutters. Thus the continual scare stories of chemical and biological weapons, for which there is no evidence that any terrorists either have them or would be able to deploy them.

Military reprisals for terrorist attacks (Libya, 1986; the Sudan and Afghanistan, 1998) killed civilians, strengthened anti-American sentiments, evidently did nothing to stop terrorism, and probably added new sympathizers to their ranks. Terrorism is a criminal and not a military activity; it cannot be erased, but it can be lessened with preventive security measures and with more attentive investigation, including the sharing of information among nations. For example, the 1993 bombing of the Trade Center might have been prevented if the FBI had translated the boxes of letters, documents, and tapes of conversations they already had in their possession. But these were in a foreign language, and the G-men couldn't be bothered.

An end to terrorism also depends on an impossibility, best articulated in a Utopian message written on a banner held by Pakistani demonstrators a few weeks ago: "America: Think About Why the World Hates You."

Rather than the attempt to apprehend the responsible criminals for trial in the World Court, we are now faced with a possible cascade of dominoes:

In Pakistan, General Musharraf has traded his support of

US military intervention for the lifting of sanctions and the prospect of millions in foreign and military aid. Yet many members of the Pakistani army are veterans of the Afghan-Russian war, or their disciples, and are sympathetic to bin Laden. To avoid a coup d'état or its own civil war, Musharraf will have to unite the country against a common enemy, which could only be India, with the battleground, as it has been for years, Kashmir. For its part, India, ruled by Hindu fundamentalists, has openly expressed its desire to follow the American example and attack Kashmiri terrorist groups, which are housed and trained in Pakistan. Both countries, of course, have atomic bombs. (During the Presidential campaign last year, Bush, when asked, could not name the leaders of Pakistan and India. Now, presumably, he knows.)

In Uzbekistan, which is admitting American troops, the Islamic Movement guerrillas trying to overthrow the dictatorial Islam Karimov will surely gain followers, which could provoke Russian intervention. The American attacks will also rally forces in the continuing Chechnya war, as well as among the Muslims leading a separatist movement in China's Xinjiang province.

Palestinian police yesterday killed Palestinian youths demonstrating in support of bin Laden. The crumbling of Arafat's authority, already in progress, will lead to the strengthening of militarist groups, which in turn will provoke further interventions by the terrifying Ariel Sharon, who has already charged the US with "appeasement" of the Arabs.

Throughout the Muslim world, the specter of American military might slaughtering helpless Afghan peasants will only fuel the rage of the youths of Radical Islam, threatening regimes from the autocratic Saudi Arabia, which bin Laden wants to overthrow for allowing the American military on sacred land, to Egypt and Turkey, which are already under threat from fundamentalist movements.

Meanwhile, the FBI, with its usual sensitivity to the public, has stated that there is now a "100% certainty" of terrorist reprisals in the US.

The War on Terrorism will be orchestrated by Vice President Cheney in the same manner in which he ran the Gulf War: in secrecy and with total control of the media. (At his press conference yesterday, Secretary of Defense Rumsfeld three times told reporters not to quote him, even though the press conference was being broadcast live on CNN.) American successes will be exaggerated—the Gulf War was reminiscent of Orwell's *1984* in its daily pronouncements of victorious triumph—but there is hope that the Western media, at least outside of the US, will not allow itself to be fooled again, and what has changed since the Gulf War is the rise of the internet as a source of instant oppositional information. It remains to be seen whether the Taliban has the media-savvy to appeal to the world's sympathies by magnifying their own casualties, or whether they will stubbornly maintain the machismo of pretending that they have not been harmed at all.

Bin Laden, however, has unexpectedly turned out to be a media genius. He has managed to indeed "terrorize" the West, and greatly magnify the perception of his actual power—which, before now, was small—by planning (or capitalizing on) the transformation of a Hollywood disaster-movie image into an unbearable reality. On the other side, his release of a tape of himself two days ago, immediately following the initiation of the bombing, was a brilliant evocation of a revered figure in Muslim tradition: the wise and ascetic saint in his cave. His message, in image and word, had the directness of television advertising, and would be impossible to refute with an equal directness: We are simple men of the faith, and they are the monsters who bombed Hiroshima and have killed a million children in Iraq and will kill us now in Afghanistan.

Bin Laden, in the tape, recalled the defeat of the Ottoman Empire. He was followed by his chief tactician, Ayman al-Zawahiri of the Egyptian Islamic Jihad, who invoked the "tragedy of al-Andalus," the expulsion of the Moors from Spain. One side believes this war began four weeks ago; the other that it is five hundred years old.

There is something more: I knew two people who died on September 11; many others were the friends of friends. Until now, they and the six thousand others were the innocent victims of an unimaginably enormous crime. But, as I watched the scenes of demonstrations around the world, I realized that they, in death, had been transformed into something else. Now they are war casualties, numbers in an increasing body count, as anonymous as the Afghans who will die from the American bombardment. No longer murder victims, they will now be portrayed, by both sides, as having died for a cause. By avenging their deaths with more deaths, Bush and Cheney and Rumsfeld and Rice and Powell are murdering the identities and, above all, the innocence of our own dead as they murder abroad.

NEW YORK: ONE YEAR AFTER

[1 September 2002]

On the verge of the first anniversary, and a commemorative media frenzy that may send the country into diabetic shock, one can either retreat to the hills like a Chinese sage, or contemplate, for a moment, from near or far, Ground Zero.

There is nothing there. The rubble has been scraped clean, so that the area now truly resembles its eponym, the Ground Zero of a nuclear attack; the empty air once occupied by the towers is almost palpable. And yet the utter nothingness of the scene is calming: a refuge of silence, an anti-memorial that is the best possible memorial, a still center around which swirls a world and a year of continual and continually mutating madnesses.

Since September 11, the American national obsession has been the delineation of how "we" are different. It seems that every magazine or newspaper article, regardless of subject—marital relations, video games, summer vacations, the new fiction—must now include at least one paragraph demonstrating how its subject, or the future of its subject, has been irrevocably transformed by that terrible day.

"We" has always been a useless generalization in a nation inhabited by a plurality of peoples who have almost nothing in common except for their taste in certain consumer goods and fast food—a taste now shared by hundreds of millions in other countries who are supposedly not "us." In fact, the word "American," when applied to anything other than the policies of the US government, is nearly always meaningless: There are too many exceptions to the rule.

Nevertheless, to indulge in this first-person plural, it is difficult to see how the artifacts and attitudes of Americans have changed at all since September 11. To take an obvious example: More people than ever went to the movies this summer to watch things getting blown up—even, in the case of *Spider-Man*, blown up in New York—movies that, according to the commentators on September 12, would never be made again, for reality had overtaken illusion. But somehow, despite disaster and expert readings of the zeitgeist, life and *Spider-Man* have a way of going on.

And yet, something is indeed different. To put it simply, "we" are the same, but we are nervous wrecks. In the last year, Americans have become like the novitiates in cults, kept awake and in a state of constant distraction. Or, more precisely, like the captured spy in 1960s movies, whose form of torture is to be tied to a chair in a small room with blaring music and images flashing on the walls.

Two powerful forces have combined to drive Americans crazy. On one side, the White House Team. (In this case one cannot, as is usual, personify and refer to an administration by the name of its leader, for George W. Bush has exactly the same relationship to the policies of his government as Britney Spears does to the operations of the Pepsi corporation.) Like all despotic governments—and I do not use the word lightly—they have recognized that the best way to solidify popular support is by exaggerating internal and external threats to society. On the other side, there is the hyperbolic and hysterical 24-hour news media, continually in need of further sensationalism to keep their audience frozen before the television. Together, the two have created a kind of techno-rave of the disturbing and the frightening, with each new artificial panic blending into the next and erasing the memory of the previous one.

We've been driven crazy because every two or three weeks for many months, the FBI or the bizarre Christian fundamentalist Attorney General, John Ashcroft, would announce that another terrorist attack was "imminent" and a "certainty" in the next few days, or this weekend, or next week. So that no American would feel complacent, the targets were spread around the country: the Golden Gate Bridge, the Sears Tower, the Lincoln Memorial, Disney World, the Liberty Bell, and even, god forbid, Universal Studios. Ashcroft, having apparently watched *The Manchurian Candidate* too many times, periodically warned of "sleeper cells" of al-Qaeda terrorists, living anonymously, maybe right next door, who could be awakened at any moment. Nearly every day, airports were evacuated, malls emptied, traffic stalled for hours crawling through checkpoints.

We've been driven crazy because, in the first weeks after September 11, the media endlessly fixated on the possibilities and consequences of terrorist biological weapon attacks, and specifically on anthrax. Predictably, this led to some thrill-seeking loner—a stock character in America—sending anthrax spores through the mail, spreading fear among all those citizens not in immediate proximity to historical monuments and theme parks. Equally predictably, the White House Team and the subservient media pronounced this to be the work of Arab terrorists, although it was obvious from the first day that the poisoned letters were being sent by one of our own Timothy McVeigh or Unabomber types—an international terrorist might release anthrax spores in the Washington Metro, but he wouldn't mail them to a celebrity-gossip tabloid popular in the supermarkets of the American provinces. (And we now know that the White House Team was so obsessed with finding an Iraqi connection that it actually forbade the FBI—which is inept enough without outside help—from pursuing domestic leads.) It still takes months for a letter sent to any branch of the government to arrive, for all their mail, like an American dinner, must be cooked in a microwave.

We've been driven crazy because the secret arrest and deportation without trial of thousands of men (the exact number is unknown) for the crime of being Middle Eastern or dark-skinned or speaking a foreign language in a public place—a group that included Israeli Jews and Indian Sikhs—was terrifying not only for Muslim Americans, but for millions of legal and illegal residents of non-European origin. Among the Latin Americans I talked with—poor people with a very hazy idea of Muslims, but an encyclopedic knowledge of immigration laws and practices—there was a general belief that it would be "first them, and then us."

We've been driven crazy because of the secret arrests; the pronouncements by Ashcroft that any criticism of the government was an act of treason; the internet postings of lists of university professors who criticized the government; the Presidential proposal to create an army of millions of government informers, composed of postmen, gas and electric meter-readers, pizza deliverymen, and anybody else who rings the doorbell; and the warnings from that Grim Reaper, Secretary of Defense Donald Rumsfeld (whom Henry Kissinger, of all people, once called "the scariest person I've ever met") about traitors among us leaking classified information, combined to provoke fears of reprisal among those with opinions to express, whether publicly or privately. After all, the bedrock of American democracy is, in theory, freedom of speech. In practice, this has meant that anyone can say anything because no one is listening. Suddenly there was the possibility that people like Ashcroft were listening, and that critics would be turned into dissidents, facing tangible repercussions for their intangible ideas.

We've been driven crazy by the wars, actual and threatened. It has been forgotten that on September 10, Bush was an extremely unpopular President. The economic boom of the Clinton years was crashing, and he was generally seen as a fool, the butt of nightly jokes by television comedians; an automaton controlled by his Dr. Mabuse/Dr. No/Dr. Evil Vice President, Dick Cheney; a President who hadn't even been elected. The only hope for Bush was a war to rally the nation, as his father had done in his own economic crisis, and it is evident that if September 11 hadn't occurred, the US would have invaded Iraq late in the year 2001. The Team began talking about it on the first day of the Bush presidency, but they needed to put the administration in place and wait for cooler weather in the desert.

September 11 gave them an alternate opportunity. Instead of treating the attack—as was done in Europe—as a monstrous crime whose perpetrators were dead but whose accomplices needed to be apprehended, it was immediately categorized as an act of war, a new Pearl Harbor, which it clearly was not. (War, as has often been said, is politics or business by other means: the attempted coercion of the other side to accept one's policies or products or sovereignty. Al-Qaeda, like all revolutionary youth movements, is more concerned with consciousness than political realities, and the Trade Center attack was a kind of hideous advertisement for itself.) In the absence of a tangible enemy with whom to wage war, the Team quickly confused al-Qaeda with the Taliban in the public mind, launched the War on Terrorism—turning a metaphor, or an advertising slogan, into a grotesque reality—

proclaimed new and thrilling victories every day, and probably slaughtered many more innocent people than died on September 11.

As for Osama bin Laden or any other important al-Qaeda member, the War on Terrorism never did, in Bush's famous John Wayne words, "smoke 'em out and hunt 'em down." But no matter: The media were delighted with the capture of a pathetic California teenager, whom they quickly named "The Rat" as they clamored for his execution, until his family hired some expensive lawyers—the American Way of Justice—and saved his life. But no matter: Ashcroft soon interrupted television programs to announce via satellite from Moscow the sensational arrest of a sinister-looking man with an Arab name who was about to explode radioactive "dirty" bombs in unnamed American cities. This led to days of televised delirium about how easy it is to make such bombs and their potential death tolls and how we can or cannot protect ourselves, until it was revealed that the nefarious dirty bomber was a Puerto Rican street gang member from Chicago who had converted to Islam in prison, and whose sinister plot had consisted entirely of looking up "radioactive bomb" on an internet search engine.

But no matter: With nothing panic-inducing coming from Afghanistan, the White House Team scanned the horizon for other places to imagine waging war. Indonesia? The Philippines? Syria? Plans were proposed, gloated over, and forgotten. Then, having already refused to support the negotiations, initiated by Clinton, between North and South Korea, the Team suddenly, out of nowhere and on the basis of nothing, began threatening to drop the Big One on North Korea—the first time the US government has ever spoken of a "preemptive first strike" with a nuclear weapon. This was followed by Bush's famous "Axis of Evil" speech—the Axis, as you may have forgotten, consisted of the closely allied nations of Iran, Iraq, and North Korea, but somehow omitted the Vandals, the Huns, and the Visigoths—which was so scary that my children seriously asked whether it wasn't a good idea to move to Costa Rica. And now, of course, the Team is waging a weird simulacrum of war in Iraq, in the manner of the tactical board games that geeks used to play before the Age of Nintendo: Every day they announce different battle strategies, complete with maps, which are followed by explanations—apparently based on telepathy—of what Saddam's defensive strategies will be.

But most of all, more than the nightmares of sleepwalking terrorists, secret police, nuclear strikes, and the junk mail of doom, in the last year we've been driven crazy by money. During the Clinton years, for the first time, the middle class put most of their savings—particularly their retirement pension savings—in the stock market. Now they have lost half of it—and in many cases, much more than half. And the collapse of the stock market has meant that many millions have either lost their jobs or must work at severely reduced wages. This, more than anything, has been devastating in a country founded on the "pursuit of happiness" and the dream of the bright future. Typically, the White House Team's solution to this crisis is to cut the taxes of those who earn more than $2 million a year. And they not only want to cut corporate taxes, but also make the cuts retroactive so that the corporations would get back the money they'd paid over the last twelve years. (As there is still supposedly an opposition party called the Democrats, they prudently chose a dozen, and not fifty or a hundred years.)

Is it possible to understand the United States? Europeans tend to think of it merely as a richer, more vulgar, and more violent version of Europe. But the two have little in common, other than large numbers of white people. The United States is a Banana Republic with a lot of money. It is perhaps the most perfect form of Banana Republic. Its generals do not have to seize power, or even concern themselves with those tedious, domestic, non-military matters, for regardless of who the ostensible leader of the government is, the generals always get what they want: lots and lots of toys to play with. (Often the Congress even gives them toys they don't want.) Moreover, like the generals of a Banana Republic, they have no great desire—since the Vietnam War—to kill people with those toys, as that might mean that some of their own boys would be killed. They're equipment fetishists, and all they want is the latest hardware and elaborate maneuvers in which to try it out. Their kind of war is Grenada, and their reluctance to go to war continues to be the greatest force for peace in the nation.

If one considers so-called "intelligence" as part of defense, approximately two thirds of the American tax dollar goes to the generals. That naturally leaves very little for anything else, which is why the US, in terms of infrastructure and general well-being, is the Banana Republic of the industrialized nations, with 25% of its children living in poverty, the worst education system, the worst mass transit, no socialized medicine, the highest rates of illiteracy and infant mortality and teenage pregnancy, homeless millions, and small cities that look as though they've just been through the plague.

Like that of any Banana Republic, the government is largely controlled by the rich. This has become even more exaggerated since the rise of the dominance of television in

American politics. One now needs vast amounts of money to buy television advertisements in order to get elected—a minor position in local government costs a million dollars, the last presidential campaign cost a billion—and those who manage to get elected must then spend the majority of their time raising the money for their re-elections. That money, needless to say, comes from the people or corporations who have it, and those people or corporations, needless to say, expect things in return. (American politics would be completely transformed overnight if television campaign advertisements were banned, as they are in most of the world, but that would entail the system voluntarily deciding to destroy itself.)

Nevertheless, before the Age of Bush, there was always the assumption that a few things had to be done for the good of the people who are actually casting the votes. This was partially because one needed those votes again, and partially because the non-elected government officials tended to come from the ranks of civil servants who, after all, had decided to dedicate their lives to serving the citizens. But Banana Republics are sometimes ripe and sometimes rotten, and this White House Team is something entirely new. Most of them, having worked for Bush Sr., spent the Clinton years in the executive offices of oil, energy, and pharmaceutical corporations. The Chief of Staff was the primary lobbyist in Washington for the auto industry against pollution controls, and Condoleezza Rice—the Team's own Xena, Warrior Princess—even has an oil tanker named after her. In the year 2000 alone, the year before they joined Junior's Board of Directors, nearly every one of them—including Colin Powell—earned between $20 and $40 million. Most have a net worth of at least $100 million, and many have much more. Considering that Bush wasn't even elected, his Team represents a corporate hostile takeover of the US government.

Let us drill into the skull of George W. Bush. His ignorance of almost everything in the world borders on the pathological. It is nearly impossible to imagine a wealthy man from an old and distinguished New England family, educated at Andover, Yale, and Harvard, who not only never thought to visit Paris, but on his first trip there this year could declare: "Jacques [Chirac] tells me the food is fantastic here, and I'm going to find out." The person he resembles most is Osama bin Laden: both the formerly dissolute sons of rich families; both called by the One God (who seems to be contradicting Himself); both cut off from the world, one in a cave and one on a ranch in the middle of nowhere; one who reads no books and the other who presumably reads one book. Is it any wonder that their families are business partners and friends? [Shortly after September 11, the only non-military plane allowed to fly was a chartered jet that left Logan Airport in Boston—the same as the hijackers—carrying eighty members of the bin Laden family back to Saudi Arabia. The conspiracy-minded may wonder how this was arranged so quickly, and before the identities, let alone the allegiances, of the hijackers were known. The link to Osama was only presumed in the following days, and only partially confirmed months later.] Bush has spent his entire life in a world as provincial as that of the House of Saud (and evidently one where France is never mentioned): a tiny circle of Texas oil and energy millionaires who repeatedly rescued him from his financial disasters because he was the President's son and a nice guy and one of them.

In the manner of patrician families, he believes, as his father did, that he and his Team know what's best for the country and the world, and they have no patience for tiresome other opinions. When they had to formulate an energy policy for the administration, they assembled a group of energy corporation executives, without bothering to include even a token environmentalist or consumer advocate or labor leader; and then they refused to release the proceedings. When they recently organized a conference to discuss the economic crisis, only large contributors to the Republican Party and small-town Republican businessmen were invited. The Team believes in Secret Government, which has been epitomized by the bizarre disappearances of Vice President Cheney-Mabuse—supposedly to protect him from terrorists, though the Team's spokesperson Bush makes frequent public appearances—which would always lead to speculation that he was dead, until he (or perhaps a double) miraculously turned up again on television. This is why they couldn't care less if the rest of the world—even their own generals—is opposed to an invasion of Iraq. They know that men must do what they have to do. On Rumsfeld's desk is a plaque with these words from that big game and small nation hunter, Theodore Roosevelt: "Aggressive fighting for the right is the noblest sport the world affords."

If you drill into Bush's skull, what you mainly find is a pool of oil. It's difficult to understand Bush—especially when he speaks—but it is somewhat easier if one realizes that he sees the whole world exclusively in terms of the production and consumption of oil. Long before September 11, he was discussing the overthrow of the Taliban so that Unocal could build a pipeline through Afghanistan from Kazakhstan to Pakistan. [Zalmay Khalilzad, the current US Special Envoy to Afghanistan—the equivalent of ambassador—was Unocal's chief consultant on the project. The so-called President of

Afghanistan, Hamid Karzai, is a former Unocal executive.]
The only country in the Western Hemisphere that has attracted his attention is Venezuela, where he tried to overthrow
Hugo Chavez, because that's where the oil is. He has no interest in Palestine and Israel, because they have no oil. Libya is
notably not a member of the Axis of Evil, because Qaddafi has
made arrangements with the oil companies. Europe is a petty
annoyance that doesn't even have any oil; Russia has oil, and
Bush said that when he looked deep into Putin's eyes he knew
he was a good man. The totalitarian nation of Saudi Arabia is
our friend because the oil flows; the totalitarian nation of Iraq
is our enemy because the oil isn't flowing as it should.

But if you drill to the core of George W. Bush's being,
there is something else, something that seems so hyperbolic,
that so smacks of the clichés of old Communist propaganda,
that it is hardly believable. And yet the evidence of his term
as the Governor of Texas, and the daily evidence of his presidency, proves that it is true. Once one clears away the rhetoric that he is handed to read out loud, it is apparent that Bush
believes that his role, his only role, as President of the United
States is to help his closest friends.

When he was Governor, he took over countless public
funds and operations, eliminated the public oversight committees, and simply handed the money or the work to his golf
buddies; laws were changed strictly for their benefit. Now
that he is President, his Team has completely re-staffed the
middle-level of the bureaucracy—the place where the day-to-
day and tangible laws are effected—and they, in turn, have
rewritten innumerable rules and regulations, not to help big
business in general, as might be expected, but as specific gifts
to the oil, energy, mining, logging, and pharmaceutical corporations run by the Bush crowd. Every day, in the back pages

of the newspaper, there is yet another story that strains credulity. I'll mention only two: No doubt at the urging of Rumsfeld, a former pharmaceutical CEO, the Team eliminated the law that required drug companies to perform separate tests on medicine that is prescribed for children—why should they spend the money? And, only a few days after it came out in the press that there were massive Enron-style accounting "irregularities" in the Halliburton Corporation when Cheney was its CEO—which he ran so badly that they paid him $45 million to leave—the White House announced that the five-year, $1.5 billion project to expand and maintain the prison at Guantanamo Bay (in expectation of more Afghan peasants to be held forever without trial) was awarded to a division of the Halliburton Corporation. One must go back to the 19th century to find this level of oblivious corruption in the White House.

After September 11, many intellectuals abroad, and many others, privately or publicly, celebrated the attack—after some perfunctory hand-wringing about loss of life—as a humiliating blow against the American Empire, and a just reward for the decades of American hegemony and aggression. One year after, it is worth remembering the concrete facts of the consequences of that day:

Because the attack happened early in the morning, the nearly 3,000 people who died were generally of three types: first, poor people—most of them black, Hispanic, or recent immigrants—who worked as janitors, handymen, food deliverers, and so on, in the towers and the adjoining buildings; second, low-ranking white-collar workers: the secretaries and junior managers and sales people who had to be in the office before the bosses arrived; and third, firemen, policemen, and other rescue workers. Very few titans of capitalism or people in power died that day.

The devastation of the downtown business area and the subsequent collapse of the tourist industry caused at least 100,000 people, most of them poor, to lose their jobs.

The secret arrests and deportations ruined the lives of some thousands of Muslim men and their families—not a single one of whom was proven to have had any connection to the hijackings—and brought continuing fear to hundreds of thousands of others.

Immigration to the US has essentially ground to a halt, with the consequent hardships to countless divided families and the millions in Third World countries who depend on the money earned by relatives in the US. Among many other specific cases, 100,000 Mexican and Canadian students who commuted to colleges and universities across the border can no longer attend classes; for the Mexicans especially, this education was their hope for decent employment.

Thousands of innocent people in Afghanistan are dead, and tens of thousands displaced. The potential deaths in Iraq or elsewhere remain to be seen.

George W. Bush, a fool on September 10, became a powerful and popular leader. He and his Team are the most globally frightening White House in modern times—far more frightening than Nixon or Reagan—and they can now do anything they want. Hardly a blow against the Empire, the Trade Center attack created one of the most arrogant and aggressive administrations in American history, one that has already demonstrated its impatience with, or repugnance for, such foundations of American democracy as free speech, open elections at home and abroad, due process of law, and the separation of church and state. And their actions will have incalculable ramifications, large and small, throughout the world, from the acceleration of global warming to the end of birth control programs in Third World villages.

For the White House Team, the hijacked planes were a blessing from the sky.

A few days ago, a man listed as one of the September 11 dead was discovered in a psychiatric hospital, a total amnesiac who has no idea what happened to him or what has happened since. On the same day, George W. Bush told an interviewer what the "saddest thing" has been about his presidency: He now only has time to jog three miles a day.

NEW YORK: SIXTEEN MONTHS AFTER

[11 January 2003]

For years they'll be debating the future of the empty pit where the World Trade Center once stood, with fantastic or hideous proposals of gardens in the sky or indoor lakes or threatening tic-tac-toe-shaped fortresses. But at the moment, the only thing certain is the fate of the actual towers themselves. The scrap steel will be shipped from the Fresh Kills landfill in Staten Island to the Grumman shipyard in Trent Lott's fiefdom of Pascagoula, Mississippi. There, it will be melted down and turned into the *New York*, an $800 million "state of the art" amphibious assault ship. In Bush America, every ploughshare must be beaten into a sword.

War and war and war. 150,000 troops are massed in the surrounds of Iraq, many of them reservists pulled from their normal lives, preparing for what the Pentagon is already declaring the "greatest precision-bombing aerial assault in history," to be followed by an invasion which the United Nations estimates will cause 500,000 casualties. There are troops or "advisers" in India, Pakistan, Uzbekistan, Kyrgzystan, Georgia, the Philippines, Colombia . . . and speculation that Iraq is merely a stop on the road to Iran.

Military operations in Afghanistan are continuing at a cost of a billion dollars a month—compared to the $25 million a month the US is spending there on humanitarian aid, most of it paying for the offices and maintenance of the aid workers, or vanishing into the crevices of local corruption. Helmeted and armored Special Forces troops still move like Robocop through the villages, past the hundreds of thousands of displaced peasants trying to survive the winter.

This year, the Pentagon budget will increase by $38 billion to almost $400 billion. The increase alone is practically the entire budget of the second-biggest military spender, China. Meanwhile, millions of Americans have lost their jobs or have had their salaries greatly reduced. There are schools around the country that will be closing a month early this year because of budget cuts, further evidence of the theory that Republicans never allot any money for education in order to keep the electorate stupid so that they'll vote for Republicans.

Everything is war and war, the talk of war, while the real, declared war—the War on Terrorism—is a complete failure. It could not be otherwise: One cannot, by definition, wage a military (and not metaphorical) war against terrorism, for the terrorists themselves are not waging a war. Wars are fought to coerce an enemy to accept one's policies or sovereignty. Even when they involve the mass slaughter of civilians—as has been increasingly the case since World War I—they are not terrorism. (A Palestinian suicide bombing, however repulsive, is the act of a civilian combatant in a war of independence.) Terrorism is committed by small, clandestine, independent groups—the evil twins of NGOs—in the attempt to persuade like-minded people to join their side, whether physically or intellectually. The massacre at the World Trade Center was, in terms of the United States, a means without an end: There were no grounds on which the US could admit "defeat"; the only possible "victory" for al-Qaeda was a sympathetic response from within the Muslim world.

In a revenge-seeking and deliberate confusion of host and guest, the US military easily overthrew the essentially unarmed Taliban regime, leaving vast areas of the country in the hands of warlords, and partially restoring the freedoms (music and television, women without burqas and girls in school, clean-shaven men) which the Afghans had enjoyed under that oppressive Soviet occupation the US, through its fundamentalist surrogates, the Taliban, had fought so long. [Freedom, however, only goes so far: A few days ago, a political cartoonist was thrown in prison for mildly satirizing President Karzai.] The country is in ruins, but the pipeline from Kazakhstan has now become a reality, and its plans are drawn, the fulfillment of an old dream among the Bush crowd. As Dick Cheney said in 1998, when he was CEO of Halliburton: "I can't think of a time when we've had a region emerge as suddenly to become as strategically significant as the Caspian. It's almost as if the opportunities have arisen overnight. The good Lord didn't see fit to put oil and gas only where there are democratically elected regimes friendly to the United States. Occasionally we have to operate in places where, all things considered, one would not normally choose to go. But we go where the business is."

The War on Terrorism has been good for business, but hasn't done anything bad against the terrorists. With one possible exception (an Egyptian strategic planner), not a single important al-Qaeda member has been killed or captured. George Bush has not mentioned the name "Osama bin Laden" in six or eight months, and no wonder: He may think he's Wyatt Earp, but those evil-doing Clanton Brothers aren't playing by the rules and they never showed up at the O. K. Corral. So all Bush can do is just shoot at anybody who looks mean.

After all, al-Qaeda—once one strips away the propaganda—appears to be a group of, at most, a few hundred educated, middle-class fanatics who masterminded terrorist actions, mainly in Africa, at the rate of one every eighteen months.

They also ran camps in Afghanistan for thousands of young peasants attracted to local jihads, including 5,000 trained by Pakistani intelligence for incursions into Kashmir and 3,000 Uzbekis attempting to overthrow the dictatorship in Uzbekistan (which receives hundreds of millions of dollars in US military aid). It is these Afghan and foreign peasants, Taliban foot soldiers and jihadis, that the Bush Team has labeled "al-Qaeda terrorists" and left to rot in Guantanamo Bay (in cages, by the way, identical to the one in which Ezra Pound was placed in Pisa in 1945). Al-Qaeda, as the recent bombings in Kenya prove, continues as it did before. Forced out of Afghanistan, it is merely less visible.

There is indeed a malevolent "sleeper cell" in the United States, but it is not the one in Attorney General John Ashcroft's apocalyptic imagination. It was formed in the 1970s, in the Ford Administration, by Donald Rumsfeld, then as now Secretary of Defense, and his young disciple, Dick Cheney, whom Rumsfeld got appointed as White House Chief of Staff. During the Reagan years they attracted brilliant young ideological extremists: Paul Wolfowitz, Richard Perle, Eliott Abrams, Zalmay Khalilzad, among them. In 1992, the last year of the Bush Sr. administration, convinced, as everyone was, that Bush would be reelected, and hoping for a second-term purge of the multilateralists surrounding the President, they launched their first secret manifesto: "Defense Planning Guidance for the Fiscal Years 1994–1999," written by Wolfowitz and Khalilzad, under the direction of then Secretary of Defense Cheney.

According to their "Guidance," with the collapse of the Soviet Union, the "first objective" of the United States was now "to prevent the re-emergence [*sic*] of a new rival":

"The US must show the leadership necessary to establish and protect a new order that holds the promise of convincing potential competitors that they need not aspire to a greater role."

"We must 'discourage' the 'advanced industrial nations' from 'challenging our leadership.'"

"We must maintain the mechanisms for deterring potential competitors from even aspiring to a larger regional or global role."

"We will retain the pre-eminent responsibility for addressing. . . those wrongs which threaten our interests. . . Various types of US interests may be involved in such instances: access to vital raw materials, primarily Persian Gulf oil; proliferation of weapons of mass destruction and ballistic missiles, threats to US citizens from terrorism . . ."

The report, which never mentioned any allies in these global efforts, was an embarrassment to Bush Sr. and his consensus-building advisers, and was quickly suppressed after it was leaked to the *New York Times.* Then Bush was defeated by Clinton, and the cell went underground in the boardrooms of corporations and right-wing foundations and think tanks.

In 1997, "appalled by the incoherent policies of the Clinton administration," they formed a group called the Project for the New American Century (PNAC), "to make the case and rally support for American global leadership" and to restore "military strength and moral clarity." Their founding statement was signed by, among others, Rumsfeld, Cheney, Wolfowitz, Khalilzad, Lewis Libby, and Jeb Bush (at the time the Heir Apparent), along with such imams of conservatism as Francis Fukuyama, William Bennett, and Norman Podhoretz.

In September 2000—when the election of Gore seemed a

certainty—PNAC produced what was to become the Hammurabic Code of the Bush Jr. Administration: *Rebuilding America's Defenses: Strategies, Forces And Resources For A New Century.* The document, which is endless, speaks openly of a "Pax Americana": expanding current US military bases abroad, and building new ones in the Middle East, Southeast Europe, Latin America, and Southeast Asia. It is contemptuous of the United Nations. It recommends "pre-emptive strikes" and particularly mentions Iraq, Iran, and North Korea. It suggests that to fight these countries we need small nuclear warheads to target "very deep, underground bunkers." (Such weapons, called Robust Nuclear Earth Penetrators, are now being developed.) It speaks of fighting and "decisively winning simultaneous major theater wars." (Thus, Rumsfeld's current obsession with taking on Iraq and North Korea at the same time.) It is the origin of that bizarre, Teutonic phrase, "homeland security." It advocates, as has now been done, pulling out of the Anti-Ballistic Missile and all other international defense treaties—in the Pax Americana we won't need them. It recommends increasing defense spending to 3.8% of the Gross Domestic Product (the amount of the 2003 budget, almost to the penny). It talks not only of controlling outer space with Star Wars weaponry, but also of controlling cyberspace, fighting "enemies" (foreign or domestic?) on the internet. One of its many charts reads:

	COLD WAR	21ST CENTURY
Security System	Bipolar	Unipolar
Strategic Goal	Contain Soviet Union	Preserve Pax Americana
Main Military Mission(s)	Deter Soviet Expansion	Secure and expand zones of democratic peace; deter rise of new great-power competitors; defend key regions; exploit transformation of war
Main Military Threat(s)	Potential global war across many theaters	Potential theater wars spread across globe
Focus of Strategic Competition	Europe	East Asia

The US, in short, is "the essential defender of today's global security order." Allies are unnecessary; world opinion is irrelevant; potential competitors must be crushed early. And, in the eeriest moment in the report, it imagines "some catastrophic event," a "new Pearl Harbor," that will be the catalyst for the US to decisively launch its new Pax. (Small wonder that, on September 12, 2001, Donald Rumsfeld insisted we immediately invade Iraq and, shortly after, Condoleezza Rice convened senior members of the National Security Council to ask them to "think about 'How do you capitalize on these opportunities?'")

The Sleeper Cell has awoken. After successfully engineering a judicial coup d'état to install their genial figurehead as President, they now control the US government. Led by Cheney and Rumsfeld, Wolfowitz is Deputy Defense Secretary, Khalilzad is Ambassador to Afghanistan, Libby is Cheney's Chief of Staff, Abrams (after having been disgraced in the Iran-contra scandal, and after years campaigning for a law to require the posting of the Ten Commandments in every government building) is now chief White House adviser on the Middle East. A half-dozen others from PNAC hold important posts in the Defense and State departments. Their goal has been cheerfully described by Condoleezza Rice (who believes that Bush is "someone of tremendous intellect"): "American foreign policy in a Republican administration should refocus the United States on the national interest. There is nothing wrong with doing something that benefits all humanity, but that is, in a sense, a second-order effect." Richard Perle, chairman of the Defense Policy Board, is more honest: "This is total war . . . If we just let our vision of the world go forth, and we embrace it entirely and we don't try to piece together clever diplomacy, but just wage a total war, our children will sing great songs about us years from now."

In ways that Ronald Reagan would envy, the Sleeper Cell is masterful at manipulating the new forms of mass media, particularly the hyperbolic television news and radio talk shows. It officially began the rhetorical invasion of Iraq precisely on September 1 (in the words of Andrew Card, White House Chief of Staff, "You don't launch a new product in August") and was relentless in creating frightening stories until the November Congressional elections. Endless reports of atrocities committed by Saddam Hussein (some of them, of course, true) were combined with assertions that, as Rumsfeld put it, there is "bulletproof evidence" linking Saddam and al-Qaeda (none of which has ever been produced), which in turn were combined with frequent warnings from Ashcroft and the FBI and the CIA of new "spectacular attacks" from al-Qaeda "that meet several criteria: high symbolic value, mass casualties, severe damage to the American economy and maximum psychological trauma."

It is dizzying trying to keep up with the news, to remember what happened the day before—which is precisely their intention—but let two examples suffice: In December, a few days after Iraq turned over a 12,000-page list of its weapons to the UN—an act first demanded by the White House, then ridiculed when Iraq complied, then partially suppressed when it revealed the names of too many US corporations that had been helping Iraq all along—the media were suddenly flooded with a story that Iraq had given al-Qaeda the nerve gas VX, an odorless, colorless oil that causes death in minutes. This story, needless to say, fit all the criteria for sensational news: Iraq/al-Qaeda connection, gruesome death, and terrorist threat. A few days later, those omnipresent and anonymous "senior officials" were telling CNN that there was "absolutely no intelligence" on this matter, "zero confirmation of evidence." Obviously, the story had originally come from the government, and it followed the classic pattern of what was, during the Vietnam War, called "disinformation": leak false information, wait until it has its effect, and then deny it, knowing that assertions remain in the collective memory longer than their negations.

Far more serious is the current frenzy over the possibility that Iraq will somehow release smallpox, either among American troops in the projected war, or in the US itself through its imagined terrorist surrogates. This has led to the mass-production of smallpox vaccines—to the delight of the drug company executives in the Bush inner circle—ambitious plans to vaccinate the entire country, and the predictable "lifeboat" debates on television of who should be vaccinated first.

The smallpox panic largely comes from the assertions of Judith Miller, a *New York Times* reporter, that unnamed "intelligence sources" are "investigating" whether a scientist named Nelja Maltseva from the Russian Institute of Viral Preparations visited Baghdad in 1990 and sold Iraq a vial of a smallpox strain that had caused an epidemic in Kazakhstan in 1972.

Dr. Maltseva died two years ago. Both her daughter and a laboratory assistant claim that she only visited Iraq once, in 1971, as part of a global smallpox eradication effort, and that her last trip abroad was to Finland in 1982. Furthermore, the Russians have always claimed that the Kazakhstan epidemic never happened, but was merely Cold War propaganda.

Edward Said attacked Miller years ago for her "thesis about the militant, hateful quality of the Arab world." Among her many books, she is the co-author of *Saddam Hussein and the Crisis in the Gulf* with Laurie Mylroie, who is the author of *Saddam Hussein's Unfinished War Against America*, which expounds the theory that Saddam personally orchestrated the 1993 World Trade Center bombing—a theory that only Richard Perle seems to believe ("splendid and convincing"). Like almost everyone on the White House Team, Miller is associated with two right-wing think tanks, the American Enterprise Institute for Public Policy Research (the latest issue of its magazine features Oriana Fallaci on the "moral superiority of Western culture") and the Middle East Forum, which has been posting the names of university professors critical of Bush on its website. The Forum is run by Daniel Pipes, who is famous for his comment about the "massive immigration of brown-skinned peoples cooking strange foods and not exactly maintaining Germanic standards of hygiene."

The general hysteria about smallpox, in other words, and the very real possibility of mass vaccinations with its statistically inevitable corresponding deaths, is entirely the result of unsubstantiated rumors published by someone with a clear agenda.

Meanwhile, over at the Pentagon, Rumsfeld has created 2POG, the $7 billion Proactive Pre-emptive Operations Group, whose "super-intelligence support activity" will combine "CIA and military covert action, information warfare, and deception." Along with the usual boys'-magazine fantasies of high-tech espionage (including something about "tagging" the clothes of terrorists with DNA samples that can be perceived by laser beams from satellites), the "proactive" component consists of "duping al-Qaeda into undertaking operations it is not prepared for and thereby exposing its personnel." That is, encouraging terrorist acts that will provoke an American response. If this seems unimaginable, or paranoid, it is worth remembering Operation Northwoods, which the Pentagon proposed to Kennedy a few months before he was assassinated. The idea then was a project of bombings, hijackings, and plane crashes that would kill American citizens and lead to popular sentiment for an invasion of Cuba. (Kennedy—even James Bond–addicted Kennedy—rejected that one.)

Around another bend of the Pentagon, the Defense Research Projects Agency has created the Information

Awareness Office, whose mission is "Total Information Awareness" (TIA). The Office is run by former Admiral John Poindexter, who in 1990 was convicted of five felony counts for lying to Congress about the Iran-contra affair. TIA, according to Poindexter, will create "ultra-large-scale, semantically rich, easily implementable database technologies" that will allow the Pentagon to access "world-wide, distributed, legacy databases as if they were one centralized database." Which means: every possible computerized record in the US, on which an individual's name appears, will be copied and collated by the Pentagon: credit card purchases, library books, police records, automatic toll-collectors on bridges, university course enlistments, membership lists, and on and on—as well as all e-mails and logs of internet surfing. They have received $200 million for a pilot program. Over the door of Poindexter's office is the motto "Scientia Est Potentia," Knowledge Is Power. (George Bush presumably being the exception that proves the rule.)

The Sleeper Cell has awoken, and there is nothing to stop them. The Democratic Party, afraid of being branded "unpatriotic" by the Republicans, has gone into hibernation. The tattered remains of the Left are—as the Left always is—more preoccupied with fighting among themselves. With a few individual exceptions, there is almost no opposition in the major media. (Powerful anti-Bush articles by, among others, Gore Vidal, Harold Pinter, and John Berger, are published in England, but not here.) The only forum for criticism is the internet, which, though still uncontrolled, remains the one point in the PNAC program that has yet to be (openly) addressed by the Bush Team. As we enter Bush II Anno III, anger has turned into a kind of sullen resignation.

Perhaps the problem is that there are no words to describe this Administration. All the pejoratives, however accurate, that might be applied—"warmongers" and "imperialists," "corrupt" and "bloodthirsty," "fanatical" and "criminal"— have been drained of their meaning by decades of propaganda. They are as banal as the rhetoric of the think tanks. Small wonder that American writers have generally been either silent or bathetic ("9/11 reminded me of the day my father died") on all that has happened in the last two years. We no longer have the words to even think about what is happening, about violence that is not "just like a movie," about people like Cheney and Rumsfeld and Perle and Wolfowitz and Rice and Ashcroft and Bush, who are not Pol Pot or Stalin or Hitler, who are lesser forms of evil, but evil nonetheless. To begin to talk about them is to relive the old nightmare of the scream with no sound.

WHERE IS THE WEST?

[14 May 2003]

The only thing that is certain about the West is that it is not the East. But in English, at least—I don't know about German—it is difficult to say where the East is. If we look at academic disciplines, we find that ancient Mesopotamia is in the Near East, but Iraq is in the Middle East: The closer it approaches in time, the further it recedes in geography. China and Japan are in the Far East, but India—despite its Eastern Religions—is not in the East at all; it's in South Asia. Orientalism is our term for Western conceptions and misconceptions of the East, but of its two classic studies, Edward Said's is about the Middle East and Raymond Schwab's is about India, and the conclusions of one do not apply to the other. And, of course, in our own time, the Cold War created a new East, one in which, from the perspective of the West, there was no difference between East Germans and North Koreans.

The only thing that is certain about the East is that it is not the West. But it is difficult to say where the West is. In many ways, it is even harder to locate than the East. It's possible to claim that for two thousand years—say, roughly 500 BCE to 1500 CE—there was a Greco-Roman-Judaeo-Christian-Islamic continuum, an interconnected, mutually nourishing, though often internally warring, civilization that was largely isolated from, and utterly unlike, the contemporary empires or large states in Mesoamerica, the Andes, China, India, and

Statement for "The Project of the West" conference, panel on "The Post-Atlantic Condition," at the Volksbuhne, (formerly East) Berlin, Germany.

sub-Saharan Africa. That may well be the only period in which Western Civilization truly existed. (And a time when where we are sitting right now was not in the West, or the East, at all, but in the North.)

After 1492, the West was permanently altered, first in its own territory by the excision of Islam, and then by its colonialist expansion into most of the rest of the world, which resulted in a range of hybrid cultures, more or less ruled by Western values, yet nevertheless excluded from anyone's idea of the West. Today the post-colonial nations of Asia may be in the East, but those in Latin America or Africa are not in the West. In fact, it's difficult to say where they are, and they tend to be excluded from discussions of the Atlantic, let alone post-Atlantic, condition, despite their coastlines.

On a round earth, the West can only be a direction, not a destination, and even then, it is far from certain where that direction leads. To take only the last fifty years, and in Europe alone, if Communism was the East, what was the West? Fascism, representative democracy, socialism, semi-socialism, or laissez-faire capitalism? Which was more Western, Denmark or Franco's Spain? One might more accurately claim that the two nations most fundamentalist in their adherence to Western ideas—albeit contradictory ideas—were Mao Zedong's China and postwar Japan.

In other words, the taxonomy has always been useless—and I've yet to mention the problem of my own little *Heimat*, the USA—and there was hope that the end of the Cold War would bring the end of it, particularly with the advent of mass migration and global communication. But this hasn't been the case. A new Orient has arisen by which some in the West are attempting to define themselves, and ironically, it is the old, not-very-far-Eastern Orient of the Islamic nations.

"They," these new/old Orientals, according to George W. Bush, "hate our values and our way of life." But those Western values, as defined and practiced by Bush himself—or more exactly, the people who tell Bush what to do and say—now include the slaughter of innocent people in distant nations that do not pose any real threat to the US; nationalistic militarism and an aestheticization of violence; laws that pertain only to members of certain ethnic groups; secret arrests, deportations, suspension of the right to legal counsel and the right to a trial; capital punishment; the equation of criticism with treason; the compilation of government dossiers on the ordinary practices of ordinary citizens; countless people now on airport security computers as potential terrorists; a President who likes to strut around in a military uniform and believes he has been given a mission by God; the proliferation of religious activity, including daily prayer meetings and Bible study groups, throughout the government of a nation founded on the separation of church and state; a massive arms buildup at the literal expense of most forms of social welfare; and an unchecked corruption that is personally enriching those closest to the presidential inner circle. In short, this new East/West "clash of civilizations," as it is called by conservatives, most resembles a fraternal argument between identical twins. [And for those who, like the perennial authority Bernard Lewis, view this clash as one between Islam and "modernity," I pose the following questions: In which country, Iraq or the United States, do 77% of the people believe that angels still visit the earth and 20% say they have personally seen one? In which country does half the population deny the theory of evolution, and entire states attempt to ban the teaching of it? In which country do 68% say that Satan is real, 20% say that Satan is not real, and 12% aren't really sure? As soon as one turns off MTV, American modernity begins to resemble a medieval monastery.]

It is quite obvious that, with the rise of Bush and the Afghanistan and Iraq wars, the North Atlantic has never been so wide—with the exception of poor England, which has become a kind of Easter Island, far from any mainland. The question is whether this is a temporary rift, brought on by the unelected junta now ruling the United States, and one that will pass when the US has—if we live long enough—another administration, or whether this junta is an extreme manifestation of permanent and irreconcilable differences between the US and Europe within what was once considered the West.

I confess that, as an outsider, I have a utopian vision of Europe. It seems to me that the two essential criteria for judging the success or failure of a government are absolute freedom of expression and the quality of life of the ordinary citizen—both of them inseparable from one another. By these standards, it may be said that most of the nations of Western Europe in the postwar period created the most perfect large-state societies in the history of mankind. Never did a factory worker have it so good, and never was he or she so free to say how bad it was.

This Utopia—despite the many imperfections in its details, which seem large to those who live in it, and small to those who view it from a distance—was, of course, among many other things, accomplished by a sense of community (national, local, and syndicalist), a minimal military, and high taxation to pay for social welfare and infrastructure, leading generally to a prosperous middle with only exceptional extremes of poverty and wealth. It was the exact opposite of the United States with its obscene military budget—about two thirds of every tax dollar—and willful neglect of social well-being, brought on by the American delusional cult of the individual. (In a recent poll, 20% of the population said they were in the top 1% of the wealthiest, and another 20% believe that they will someday be there.) The result, as everyone knows, is that the US has enough nuclear weapons to destroy the entire earth seven times over and enough conventional weapons to wage permanent war, and the worst education, mass transit, health care, work benefits, infant mortality, literacy rate, and level of homelessness among the technological nations.

To an outsider, it seems that the European Utopia is beginning to fall apart just as it is on the verge of its greatest triumph. On one side, the European Union, which has the potential to serve as a model for many parts of the world, and which—despite all the flaws in the machinery—is a very moving coming-together of nations in what has been, for many centuries, perhaps the most barbaric and bloodthirsty place on earth.

On the other side, the almost-perfect social system is beginning to be dismantled in many countries, largely because of resentment toward their immigrant or non-white populations. They are reenacting the Reaganism which effectively transformed the US into the wealthiest Third World country through its belief that it was better to demolish services than to offer them to those who were considered unworthy of receiving them. This is not the place to discuss immigration, but I'd like to mention, in passing, two things. The European Union only became possible as the populations of the individual nations became less homogenous; Euro-consciousness begins when it is no longer possible to define the French or Germans or Italians. Secondly, speaking as a literary writer, immigration has been a tremendous force in the revitalization of the literatures of the Western European languages: new people bringing new stories, new perceptions, and new ways of expressing them. And this is true in all the arts: From a cultural point of view, immigration has been the salvation of Europe.

It may well be, as some have written, that the US, in the moment of its most grandiose imperial dreams, is actually at the beginning of the end of its empire. As an American, I hope the next generation will live in a world where the USA is just another country. But as a utopian, I think this will best come about not through a bellicose anti-Americanism in the rest of the world, but through the positive influence of a new kind of non-Americanism.

What would the world be like if Europe just stopped playing the American game? If Europe, as the non-America, no longer sold arms to the Third World, and sent only humanitarian aid? If Eastern Europe refused to buy all the American military junk that NATO requires? (Or even better: if Europe kicked the US out of NATO altogether, and transformed it into a pan-European peacekeeping force?) If Europe, as the non-America, actively promoted environmental protections and reproductive rights throughout the world? If European ingenuity were directed toward developing alternate energies that would liberate us all from this short and doomed and bloody Age of Oil? If Europe exerted its diplomatic skills in the warring parts of the globe and peace talks were not dependent on American whims and lobbyists?

It seems to me that the optimistic Euro-consciousness, particularly among the young, that began with the creation of the EU has been revitalized by anti-Americanism, by its awareness of how different is the world that Europeans inhabit. It will be an enormous missed opportunity if this sentiment never goes beyond anti-Americanism, particularly now when, for at least another generation, there will be so many nations that distrust or actively loathe the US.

George Bush has said—and he actually said this—that "We will export death and violence to the four corners of the earth in defense of our great nation." It must be assumed that, for the foreseeable future, the United States will be the cause of wars, civil unrest, economic exploitation, and environmental disaster. This is the moment when Europe could be a counter-force, exporting its ideas and practices of social justice and state welfare, disarmament, freedom of expression, and culture as a source of national pride. Gandhi famously said that Western civilization would be a good idea. We need to get beyond East and West and start thinking about world civilization, which would also be a good idea. This is a long road, but it seems to me that, right now, the only place with the wealth and the technology where this road could begin is in a unified, multi-ethnic Europe.

TWO YEARS AFTER

[11 September 2003]

Could you comment on the second anniversary of the terrorist attack on the USA and the beginning of this period which has extremely affected the world?

I live in downtown New York City, and every day I look at the empty space where the Twin Towers once stood. Many of us had hoped that this—the first mass slaughter on US soil since the Civil War of the 1860s—would effect a profound change in the way Americans think about the world and think about violence, among many other things. But this has not happened at all.

It should have been a force for peace. Instead, television turned it into a "tragedy" only slightly more grave than the death of Princess Diana. It gave the radical ideologues who form the Bush junta carte blanche to enact all the things they've been dreaming of for years: the invasions of Afghanistan and Iraq, the creation of an imperial Pax Americana, the withdrawal from international treaties, and the dismantling of countless domestic laws relating to environmental protection, fair labor practices, the rights of women, and civil liberties. It turned the victims in New York into casualties of war. And, above all, many thousands of other innocents in Afghanistan and Iraq are now dead or their lives are ruined.

Excerpts from an e-mail interview with Igor Lasic of *The Feral Tribune*, Belgrade, Croatia. Some questions and answers from interviews at the same time with the Mexican newspapers *Reforma*, *La Jornada*, and *El Financiero* have also been added.

85

Numerous indications show that the presidency of George W. Bush put into action what you call the "Sleeper Cell" of the American extreme right. Could you comment on the claims that the present government not only took advantage of the terrorist attacks but also encouraged them directly or at least did not want to stop them.

The attack on the World Trade Center was the best thing that could have happened to the Bush Team, but I do not believe any of the conspiracy theories which have become so popular throughout the world. They are dependent on a belief in the omnipotence of American intelligence agencies. It's difficult for the world to understand that these agencies are, in fact, hopelessly inept: bloated bureaucracies in a state of paralysis. These people were plainly incapable of carrying out a coordinated and successful mission—which, after all, 9/11 was.

The so-called American "war against terrorism" is becoming a more dangerous global problem than terrorism itself.

Most people in the world now believe that the US is the world's greatest threat to peace. South Koreans believe it is more dangerous than North Korea. They are completely right. Terrorism is a criminal activity that must be dealt with by police and intelligence activity—as has been done in Western Europe. The military slaughter of innocent peasants in Afghanistan did nothing to stop terrorism. The invasion and occupation of Iraq has nothing to do with terrorism, as everyone knows, despite the claims of the Bush Team. In fact, for those who like conspiracy theories, it is worth pointing out that Bush has accomplished two of the primary goals of Osama bin Laden: the overthrow of the secular Saddam Hussein and the withdrawal of US troops from Saudi Arabia.

And the Iraq war has recruited more al-Qaeda members and sympathizers than 9/11. Iraq, very much like the Spanish Civil War, has become an international cause, with foreigners volunteering to fight. One might say that Bush has become a more effective leader of al-Qaeda than Osama.

When the USA entered World War II, it had an enormous support both at home and abroad, and after the war, it was for decades a democratic and cultural ideal for the whole world. Since the war in Iraq, the situation has deeply changed, and America has gained a very bad reputation all over the world, which will have far-reaching effects.

I'm not so sure that the USA was a "democratic ideal" to much of the world during the Vietnam War, and in the countless countries where it overthrew legitimate governments. Nevertheless, it is quite true that anti-Americanism has never been so strong. And justifiably so. But I would say that in the West in general, and among cosmopolitan people in Muslim and Third World countries, the necessary distinction is made between America and the unelected government that now rules it. Anti-Americanism today is really anti-Bushism.

Thirty years before the attack on the WTC, on September 11, 1973, Salvador Allende, the legally elected President of Chile, was overthrown by Pinochet and his military junta, assisted by the USA, or more precisely, by President Nixon's government. Do you see any connection between the two events?

Only in the sense that September 11, 2001, has deep roots in the decades of the Cold War that was responsible for the overthrow of Allende. Al-Qaeda would not have existed if the US had not supported the House of Saud and its promotion of Wahhabism in the 1950s and 1960s as a bulwark against "socialist" and nationalist movements in the Middle East, and if the US had not armed and trained the Afghan "mujahadeen" against the Soviet occupation.

In America today an official left opposition or a formal democratic alternative to the present government hardly exists—the opposition is just a little less right-wing than the far-right government—while the political life is strictly controlled. Is there, in your opinion, a possibility for a change any time soon?

The Democratic Party is slightly to the right of a European conservative party, and the Republicans are slightly to the left of a National Front party. I, for one, have never voted "for" a candidate, I only vote against the worse alternative. Campaigns are dependent on television advertising, which are enormously expensive. The money must come from somewhere, and the people who give the money naturally expect something in return. American politics would be transformed overnight if, as in many European countries, television advertising were banned. The other problem is Washington, DC, itself—a kind of Brasília, an artificial capital cut off from the rest of the country. American politicians inhabit a sealed environment of bureaucrats and lobbyists, and never see the real effects of the laws they create. We'd have a very different government if the capital were in New York or Chicago, or somewhere where ordinary citizens live. In short, I don't expect anything to change.

However, there is a strong anti-war opposition in the USA, mostly outside of the institutions. It is ignored by the Bush's government, but it can't abolish it.

There are many, many people unhappy with the Bush government, and their numbers are growing every day as the economy gets worse and as Americans continue to die in the hopeless disaster of the Iraq occupation. Until now, the primary forum for their discontent has been the internet. Lately, however, the Democrats are waking up to the fact that there are so many unhappy people, and that they might vote for Democrats in the next election. So, for the first time, we are hearing some criticism—or at least some skepticism—in official politics. The remarkable support for Howard Dean—whom no one had ever heard of a few months ago—is evidence, whatever the result, that at least some people are eager to have something that resembles a two-party system again. But things change so quickly in the hysteria and instant amnesia of the mass media that it is impossible to predict how long this will last.

To what extent is the American public aware of the fact that the wars of George W. Bush are not only unscrupulous aggression and occupation, but also a direct reflection of the capital which is spreading and firming its position in the world, because the American economy cannot win the market struggles in some other way?

Ha! It is difficult to underestimate America's near-total ignorance of the rest of the world. Outside of certain nomadic tribes in the rain forests and deserts, there is no more insular society on earth. 20% of American high school students cannot find the USA on a world map. 30% can't find the Pacific

Ocean, including probably a lot of people who live on the coast of the Pacific Ocean. Only 7% of university students study a foreign language. The total number of translations of literary books—fiction, poetry, plays, essays, criticism—published by all presses, large and small, in the US each year is 250. (UNESCO, commenting on the "insularity" of the Muslim world, noted that every year only 300 books are translated into Arabic.)

How do you explain the fact that there is still no official and convincing evidence of illegal arms in Saddam Hussein's regime, which was an excuse for the war in Iraq?

Obviously there never were any weapons of mass destruction in Iraq—or hadn't been since the Gulf War. The Pentagon was getting all its "intelligence" about the weapons and the anti-Saddam sentiments of the people from Ahmad Chalabi. I suspect that Rumsfeld and Cheney and Wolfowitz and company knew that the WMDs and the imminent nuclear capability and the ties to al-Qaeda were absolute lies. But the great mystery is why they believed—and I think they genuinely believed it—that Chalabi would be welcomed by the Iraqi people as the Great Liberator and easily installed as a puppet President. He even promised them an oil pipeline to Israel! This despite the fact that he was a convicted embezzler who hadn't been in the country since he was a teenager, and was considered a loose cannon by the CIA. It was evident the day he finally arrived in Iraq that he had no following at all outside of London, if even there.

Assuming that all the official explanations are untrue, how do you explain the invasion of Iraq? Was it all about oil?

Well, of course it had nothing to do with 9/11 or terrorism. I believe that if 9/11 had not occurred, the US would have invaded Iraq in the winter of 2001–2. All the plans were in place in the first weeks of the Bush Administration. But I think the reasons for the invasion were a "perfect storm" of factors, and cannot be reduced to a single factor, like oil. These included: a distraction from the disastrous economic news; fears of the collapse of the House of Saud and the need to have both a new source for Middle Eastern oil and a place for US military bases; the openly imperialistic ambitions of the ideologues from the Project for a New American Century around Bush (including Rumsfeld, Cheney, Rice, Wolfowitz, Perle, and many others); a national rallying behind the President to ensure the success of the Republicans in the 2002 Congressional and eventually the 2004 Presidential elections; the long-term threat of the euro as a viable alternative to the dollar and the very real possibility that the UN sanctions against Saddam would be lifted (since he had no WMDs) and that he would start selling his oil for euros; and finally, the very complex Bush family drama, where the prodigal son needed not only to prove his worth to his father, but succeed where his father had failed, in eliminating Saddam.

What do you think will happen in Iraq?

Iraq is a disaster, and such a classic "quagmire" situation that if Mahatma Gandhi were elected the President of the United States tomorrow, he would have difficulty withdrawing the troops. Since Bush's famous "Mission Accomplished" stunt—the aircraft carrier was just off the coast of California, and they had to turn it back to sea so he could land in his little jet—more American soldiers have died than during the actual "war," and they are continuing to die every day. (By the way, Bush is the first American President to strut around in a military uniform. Even Eisenhower, the war hero, never wore his while he was President. What national leaders wear uniforms? Hitler, Stalin, Mussolini, Pinochet, Mobuto, Qaddafi, Saddam, Castro . . .)

Among many other things, the US failed to realize that, because of the sanctions, the Baath Party had evolved into a complex system of patronage that could not be dismantled overnight—resulting now in a total breakdown of every aspect of the infrastructure—and that, the Kurds apart, the only anti-Saddam political leaders with a genuine power base are the Shi'ite imams—precisely whom they don't want to run the country.

It is clear from the recent bombings of the water supplies, the UN headquarters, and the Shi'ite mosques, that the Americans have set off an extremely complicated civil war which they don't understand and will never be able to control. The war in Iraq has only just begun, and it's much worse than Vietnam. There, at least, the Americans had someone to lose to.

Very few American intellectuals who openly oppose Bush appear in the mass media. Could you explain this?

Are there any? It is difficult for people in other countries to understand that the US does not have public intellectuals. Poets and novelists write poems and novels, critics appear in academic journals and forums. With very rare exceptions, they do not publish in newspapers or mass-circulation magazines, do not appear on television, and are almost never interviewed. This is the normal situation: The US is the only country on earth that has never taken pride in its cultural producers.

It may be the only country without a Minister of Culture. So it is no surprise that the mass media has been closed to anti-war intellectuals. Nevertheless, writers do have an outlet through the internet—the only source for opposition news and information in the US—but their public sense has been so atrophied it doesn't even occur to them that they might have something to say. 10,000 poets wrote poems against the war, but I don't know of one who wrote an essay or article.

It is noteworthy that there were no photographs of the people killed at the World Trade Center, while the pictures of Saddam's dead sons and of Afghan Taliban corpses flew around the world. How do you feel about this double standard?

More obscene than the photos of Saddam's sons were their murders. The US used to believe in bringing criminals to justice, as in the Nuremberg trials, not merely assassinating them. (And Bush has often remarked that he wants Saddam dead, not arrested.) But this question has no simple answer. Americans, unlike Europeans, have never seen images of the victims of the Iraq war, just as people in the Middle East never saw images of the victims of the Trade Center attack. On the one hand, it is a violation of the personal privacy of the dead and their families; on the other, a graphic demonstration of the tangible results of violence inserts some reality into the clouds of rhetoric.

How has the media changed in the USA since 9/11?

Chairman Mao never created such brilliant propaganda as is seen every day on American television. The heroic rescue of Private Lynch, her body riddled by bullets and stab wounds, raped by her captors. (Well, actually, she was in a car crash, and her kindly American-trained Iraqi doctors tried to give her back, but the US soldiers fired on the ambulance.) The thrilling populist toppling of Saddam's statue, which was repeated in an endless loop like some installation artwork. (Well, actually an American tank pulled it down in a sealed-off plaza where 150 Chalabi supporters, flown in the day before, were told to celebrate before the cameras.) The terrifying mobile biological weapons laboratories. (Well, actually, they were used to make weather balloons.) And on and on.

All news refers to the Great Leader. I happened to tune in to CBS on the day of the UN headquarters bombing in Baghdad and a major suicide bombing in Jerusalem. The news report began: "In spite of the President's efforts to bring peace to the Middle East, violence rocked the region today."

There's even been a made-for-television movie about Bush's heroism on 9/11, with Bush ludicrously barking orders at Cheney and Rumsfeld (instead of them telling Georgie to "Go fetch") and lecturing Condoleezza on—if you can believe this—"pluralism and modernity." An actor portrays Bush. Only one other national leader commissioned movies with actors playing himself, and that was Stalin. But this is the USA and not the Soviet Union: Before 9/11, the actor portraying the Supreme Commander used to play Bush as a complete idiot on a satirical comedy show. Stalin would never have stood for that.

Bush has been quoted as saying: "You know, I had a drinking problem. Right now, I should be in a bar in Texas, not the Oval Office. There is only one reason that I am in the Oval Office and not in a bar: I found faith. I found God. I am here because of the power of prayer."

Bush's religion should be a personal matter. What is frightening is that he has brought it to a government founded on the separation of church and state. A true Christian like Jimmy Carter never created prayer meetings and Bible study groups in every branch of the government, never referred to Jesus in official statements, never turned over government duties to missionary groups, and never insisted that the moral strictures of the Christian right become law in the rest of the nation and practice in the rest of the world.

But who can know the ways of God? According to their testimonies, He both commanded Bush to invade Iraq and Osama to attack the Twin Towers. What was He thinking? And why didn't He leave Bush in that bar? The next thing, He'll strike us all with boils.

BUSH THE POET

[9 January 2004]

In October 2003, back from a junket to Russia and France (where Chirac, that scamp, boldly kissed her on the hand), Laura Bush, with George at her side, inaugurated the National Book Festival in Washington:

> President Bush is a great leader and a husband, but I bet you didn't know he is also quite the poet. Upon returning home last night from my long trip I found a lovely poem waiting there for me. Normally I wouldn't share something so personal, but since we're celebrating great writers, I can't resist.

> Dear Laura,

> Roses are red,
> Violets are blue,
> Oh my lump in the bed,
> How I've missed you.

> Roses are redder,
> Bluer am I,
> Seeing you kissed
> By that charming French guy.

> The dogs and the cat,
> They missed you too,
> Barney's still mad you dropped him,
> He ate your shoe.

The distance, my dear,
Has been such a barrier,
Next time you want an adventure,
Just land on a carrier.

Exegetes revealed that "lump in the bed" is Boy George's term of endearment for his wife and, in a weird bit of Karl Rove damage control, that it was actually George and not Laura who had accidentally dropped Barney the dog when he greeted her on the tarmac after her trip. (You can't have a butterfingers Prez on the nuclear button.)

Clearly the barrier/carrier rhyme of the last stanza was beyond the President's verbal skills and, at the time, I wrote: "Not merely another Bush Stupidity story. It becomes apparent that Little George didn't even write this banality, which makes the whole scene more perverse."

Three months later, on December 28, Laura appeared on NBC's *Meet the Press*:

MR. RUSSERT: Books and learning—Mrs. Bush, you're a teacher, a librarian. You also helped create the National Book Festival. And I believe we have an opportunity here to watch you addressing a group after returning from Russia and France. And you talked about someone who I didn't know wrote poetry, but let's listen:

[Videotape of National Book Festival address—tellingly omitting the first sentence where Laura specifically attributes the poem to George.]

MR. RUSSERT: Now, who could have written that poem, huh? I mean, what . . .

MRS. BUSH: Well, of course, he didn't really write the poem. But a lot of people really believed that he did. That evening at the dinner, what some woman from across the table said: "You just don't know how great it is to have a husband who would write a poem for you."

The Bushes are famous jokers. (Bush Sr. liked to shake hands with a joy buzzer, and on his first day in the Oval Office he delighted visitors with a calculator that squirted water.) But in this case, it's difficult to untangle who is playing the joke on whom. George on Laura—with the compliant lump in the bed and dog-dropping fall gal demeaning herself by publicly "sharing" it? Laura on George, "quite the poet"—making a fool of her hub for something she knows he didn't do (even if it blames her for something she didn't do)? An unknown third party—tricking Laura into believing the poem is George's? Or both George and Laura on the audience—to emphasize that, at an event honoring "books and learning," the President of the United States, as a regular guy, has little to do with either? The heart of another is a dark bush.

The peculiar pathology of the Bush family—all of them, including Laura, who for no reason is usually considered an exception—is that everything they do or say, no matter how trivial, usually turns out to be fake or a lie. Laura reads a poem by the President to a bunch of book-huggers; the press widely reports the poem as Presidential; and months later she giggles that it wasn't by Junior at all . . . Or the Thanksgiving turkey that Soldier George "served" to the troops in Iraq, which was not edible. It had been doctored by a food stylist for the photo shoot, and presumably carried over on Air Force One. ("OK, Condi, we're here. Where's that goddam bird?")

Or, on that same Excellent Adventure, the story about the British Airways pilot startled by the sight of the Presidential Plane whizzing through the clouds. They made that one up too, though it's sure to appear in the tv movie. Next thing we'll hear is that it wasn't even Bush in Iraq, but one of the doubles he employs for fund-raising appearances while he plays pinocle with Cheney down in the Code Orange Spider Hole.

Meanwhile, the mystery lingers. Who did write that poem? Wolfowitz? Perle? Rumsfeld? Dana Gioia?

A FEW FACTS & QUESTIONS
[2 February 2004]

One of the enduring mysteries is what it takes for news to become news in the US. All the recent scandalous revelations about the Bush Team and the war in Iraq have been common knowledge or open secrets for months or years. Yet even now they are disappearing into clouds of denial, recrimination, and deliberate obfuscation. Administration officials wear out the old waters-in-Casablanca line ("I was misinformed"), while the hawks and so-called liberal hawks take recourse in selecting and refuting the most specious of their opponents' arguments. A few plain facts:

1. The invasion of Iraq was a priority of the Bush Team from the very beginning. [On January 27, 2001, I wrote that a "principal concern" of the new Administration would be a "return to Iraq." I got my insider information from the *New York Times*.] All of the solemnly and endlessly repeated warnings of imminent threats, terrorism, and WMDs were merely a marketing scheme—as Paul Wolfowitz has admitted—for the plans they had made long before.

2. Iraq had no weapons of mass destruction. The current crosshatch of finger-pointing over "who knew what" is mere damage control in an election year. On the matter of chemical/biological weapons, the Bush Team selected what they wanted to hear from the CIA, while complaining that the CIA was underestimating the threat. (Now they are falsely complaining that the CIA overestimated the threat.) To counter the information they didn't like, Rumsfeld created his own, unprecedented intelligence office within the Pentagon to confirm his delusions. All the intelligence sources (including the Israelis) were quite clear that Iraq did not have nuclear weapons, or even the rudiments of potential nuclear capability. The nukes were the fabrication of Ahmad Chalabi and of other Iraqi exile groups, which the Bush Team enthusiastically accepted despite the lack of evidence, and which they used as their most compelling argument for immediate invasion. While most of the Team is now blaming the CIA for misinformation, Dick Cheney is sticking to his disinformation. Just last week, he emerged from one of his bird-slaughtering junkets to claim that Iraq did indeed have mobile biological weapon laboratories—the same labs whose function was proven, months ago, to be the manufacturing of helium for weather balloons.

[An aside: Everyone got a good laugh when Bush, in the State of the Union address, gravely charged that Iraq had "weapons of mass destruction-related program activities." (As the comedian Jon Stewart said, "What the fuck is that?") Susan Stranahan of the *Columbia Journalism Review* has tracked down the origin of the phrase to an interim report last October by David Kay, the head weapons inspector for the Iraq Survey Group, who now states that Iraq had no WMDs. In testimony before the Senate Armed Services Committee, he was asked what the phrase means:

"That includes, for example . . . a program to develop a substitute for a major precursor for VX using indigenous production capability and indigenous chemicals so they would not have to import it. It includes a study, for example, on a simulant for anthrax . . . They [the Iraqis] had looked at lethality of various agents and classified them. That's WMD-related work."

Well, ok . . . So another Senator asked: "How many countries would you say in the world today would qualify under the category of developing weapons of mass destruction-related program activities, or having such activities?"

Kay replied: "Probably about 50."

Which leaves 49 more countries to preemptively invade.]

3. Saddam Hussein was monstrous. However, most of his monstrous acts occurred in the 1980s, when he was an ally of the US—a bulwark against Iranian fundamentalism—with biological, chemical, and other weapons supplied by the US, or immediately following the Gulf War. According to many reports from those inside (most vividly, his personal translator), Saddam in the last years was in "autumn of the patriarch" mode: holed up in his palaces writing his trashy novels, and oblivious to the details of government. The regime was on the verge of collapse—but, thanks to the trade embargo, had been kept in power by its strict control over food, medicine, and other essentials. "Regime change" in Iraq would have occurred, and probably in the near future, without the US invasion.

4. The invasion of Iraq was not, as the liberal hawks claim, an act of humanitarian intervention. Although the regime was oppressive—like many others in the world today—Saddam's most grotesque acts had occurred years before. The comparisons to Kosovo or Rwanda are false: The invasion did not stop any slaughter, it led to one.

The liberal hawk argument that we should celebrate the end of a fascist government relies on a selective reading of history. While it is true that the Baath Party, like many nationalist movements, was founded in the 1940s based on European fascism, these same hawks do not—to take one example—similarly advocate the overthrow of the government of India, currently ruled by the BJP Party (the direct descendent of the RSS, the assassins of Gandhi, who attempted to ally themselves with Hitler—though Hitler, in the matter of India, preferred British rule). It may be said that more innocents are now dying in India because of government complicity than died in recent years in Iraq, before the war—but those Indian innocents are, of course, Muslims. Furthermore, the humanitarian intervention argument bizarrely and willfully ignored who was doing the intervening. If, say, the Argentine junta had invaded Chile and overthrown Pinochet, would they have celebrated the end of the Chilean dictatorship?

5. The Bush Team sincerely believed that, after overthrowing Saddam, they could easily set up a puppet government under Chalabi, who would be welcomed as a liberator, and they could get on with the serious business of reconstruction and drilling for oil. A "piece of cake," as they notoriously said. There appear to have been no plans at all, other than business plans, for the occupation.

6. We are now at the beginning of what may well be a very long civil war in Iraq. The Kurds, after their semi-independence during the embargo, do not want to be returned to an Iraqi state. The Sunni minority is rightfully fearful of a rule by the Shi'ite majority, after decades of Sunni repression. The Shi'ites, quite brilliantly, have called the American bluff by demanding democracy—immediate direct elections—which is the last thing the US wants, as it would undoubtedly lead to a state ruled by mullahs and unfriendly to American business. Iraq, an invention of the Versailles Treaty that was only held together by colonial or totalitarian governments, is Yugoslavia.

7. More American soldiers have died or have been wounded since the "Mission Accomplished" end of the war than during it. The capture of Saddam did not lessen the violence, or essentially change anything at all, proving his ultimate irrelevance to what is happening right now.

AFGHANISTAN & TERRORISM

8. Terrorist acts are performed by tiny groups of individuals who are often transformed in the popular imagination (as in the 1960s or in the Muslim world today) into outlaw-heroes. Military activity, with its inevitable killing of civilians, not only does not stop terrorism, but it recruits further individuals to the cause, in the name of protecting or revenging innocents against the aggressor. Terrorism can only be fought through police and intelligence agencies. Europe arrests suspected terrorists; the US blows up the neighborhood where it thinks they live.

9. The war in Afghanistan killed thousands of innocents and did nothing to stop al-Qaeda and its fellow travelers, as the subsequent bombings in other countries proved. The camps that trained peasant foot soldiers for fighting in Kashmir and Uzbekistan may indeed be destroyed (if they have not merely relocated to Pakistan), but there is no evidence that the cells of middle-class, educated terrorists have been weakened, and much speculation that they have been strengthened.

10. The Taliban were monstrous. However, in their absence, the country has largely returned to warlord rule, with the "democratic" government limited to Kabul and its immediate environs. Outside of Kabul, the rights of women have not improved (or even, as it is never said, approach the freedom women held under the Soviet occupation—or, for that matter, in Iraq under Saddam). Poppy production, banned by the Taliban, has once again become the country's largest industry. Radio music may be back, but the subsistence economy is even worse, and the Taliban are regrouping on the other side of the Pakistan border. Afghanistan—that elephant's graveyard of empires—is now a forgotten disaster.

11. There was absolutely no connection between al-Qaeda and Saddam Hussein. (Osama bin Laden, after all, had often called for the overthrow of the secularist Saddam. And one of Saddam's last messages to his followers was a warning against the Islamists.) Saddam had nothing to do with international terrorism, and Iraqi Baathism under Saddam was a strictly national totalitarian movement without (Kuwait aside) the international ambitions of radical Islam. Everyone on the Bush Team knew this from the beginning. Their conflation of Saddam and terrorism, which still continues, is a lie that has led to many thousands of deaths.

12. The War on Terrorism has successfully created the climate of fear (the color-coded Alerts, the duct tape, the repeated use of the word "terror" in Bush's State of the Union address, etc.) that is a traditional hallmark of a totalitarian state. It has created chaos among foreigners living in the US, Muslim Americans, and anyone attempting to visit, study in, or emigrate to the US. It has created the largest new government bureaucracy—the Department of Homeland Security—since the New Deal, and surely the most useless one. It has created countless petty annoyances in airports, office buildings, public gathering places. It has suspended the legal rights of citizens and resident aliens, and destroyed the lives of innocent people through deportations and secret arrests.

The one thing the War on Terrorism has not done is eliminate terrorists. The invasions of Afghanistan and Iraq have generally alienated the Muslim (and the rest of the) world from the US, and have created countless new sympathizers of radical Islam. Only a very few of those, of course, will become active terrorists, but terrorism depends on only a few.

13. Nearly everything said by the Bush Team (or their spokesperson, the President) has turned out to be a lie. Every day yet more lies are revealed: There are so many of them that the word "lie" has lost all meaning. By the standards of the Republicans during the Clinton Administration (Whitewater, Monica, Travelgate) the President and Vice President should be impeached, and every important member of the Administration forced to resign.

We can imagine what the Republicans would have done if a Democratic Administration:

—had leaked the name of a covert CIA operative in petty revenge;
—awarded former employers billion-dollar contracts without competitive bidding and then allowed them to grossly inflate prices;
—ignored intelligence about terrorist threats before 9/11;
—failed to apprehend the anthrax killer;

—run up a $500 billion deficit for the coming year, thanks to massive government spending;

—was losing 5–10 American soldiers a week in Iraq, keeping the wounded invisible (and cutting their medical benefits), while offering no possible exit scenario;

—refused to prosecute its biggest campaign contributor for cheating consumers out of billions of dollars;

—failed to capture Osama bin Laden;

—had an education policy based on falsified state statistics from the time when the current President was Governor;

—hacked into the computers of the rival party for more than a year, stealing strategy plans;

—set up an internet gambling racket for "terrorism futures" at the Pentagon;

—refused to reveal the names of those who had attended important policy meetings;

—had the CEOs of voting machine manufacturing companies running their campaign committees;

—presided over the greatest job loss since the Great Depression (while proclaiming an economic recovery);

—circumvented Constitutional mandates by appointing ideological judges during a Congressional recess;

—frequently announced the "certainty" of an "imminent" terrorist attack "within days";

and on and on. It's safe to say there would be nobody left in office.

14. The Democrats, and their candidates for President, should be presenting concrete information that reveals the multiplicity and depth of these lies and deceptions. Instead they are speaking platitudes worthy of the politico poobahs in a

Preston Sturges movie, using the bankrupt rhetoric of former campaigns ("special interests," "I'm an outsider"), or attacking each other for positions held years ago. It is difficult to imagine how they could not lose.

Nevertheless, if the election seems at all close, there will doubtlessly be another imminent security threat or another foreign invasion in early October, causing the nation to rally around the President in time of crisis. It is unimaginable, or all too imaginable, what another four years of this ruling junta will bring.

REPUBLICANS: A PROSE POEM

[12 August 2004]

"They hate our friends. They hate our values.
They hate democracy and freedom, and individual liberty."
President George W. Bush

Thomas Donahue, Director of the US Chamber of Commerce, is a Republican. He said the newly unemployed should "stop whining."

Alfonso Jackson, Secretary of Housing and Urban Development, is a Republican. He explained the enormous cuts to low-income housing by saying, "Being poor is a state of mind, not a condition."

Rick Santorum, Senator from Pennsylvania, is a Republican. He defended cuts to child care and welfare by suggesting that "making people struggle a little bit is not necessarily the worst thing."

Eric Bost, Undersecretary of Food and Nutrition, US Department of Agriculture, is a Republican. A study by his own agency said that 34 million Americans, including 13.6 million children under the age of 12, were affected by hunger, but Bost doubts these numbers: "If you ask any teenager if they're happy about the food they have in their house, what will they say?" Responding to a report that the number of people seeking assistance at food pantries in Ohio had increased by 44% in the last three years, Bost told an Ohio newspaper: "Food pantries don't require documentation of income. . . so there's no proof everyone asking for sustenance at a soup kitchen is truly in need."

Dr. Tom Coburn, former Congressman and current candidate for the Senate from Oklahoma, is a Republican. He said that lesbianism is so rampant in Oklahoma high schools that girls are only allowed in the bathroom one at a time, though no high school could be found where this has occurred. Dr. Coburn supports the death penalty for doctors who perform abortions.

Republicans do not like dogs. Major General Geoffrey Miller, former Chief of Prisons at Guantanamo Bay, now Director of Prisons in Iraq, said that "at Guantanamo Bay we learned that the prisoners have to earn every single thing that they have. They are like dogs and if you allow them to believe at any point that they are more than a dog then you've lost control of them."

Republicans like dogs. Trent Lott, Senator from Mississippi, was asked about the use of attack dogs in torturing an Iraqi prisoner. He replied that there's "nothing wrong with holding a dog up there unless it ate him."

Republicans have a sense of history. The National Museum of Naval Aviation now exhibits the actual Navy S–3B Viking fighter jet that carried the President to the deck of the USS *Abraham Lincoln* for his "Mission Accomplished" speech. It has "George W. Bush Commander-in-Chief" stenciled just below the cockpit window.

Republicans are fighting terrorism. Rod Paige, Secretary of Education, called the National Education Association, with a membership of 2.7 million teachers, a "terrorist organization." Karen Hughes, adviser to the President, said that, especially after September 11, Americans support Bush's efforts to ban abortion because "the fundamental issue between us and the terror network we fight is that we value every life."

Patricia "Lynn" Scarlett, Assistant Secretary of the Interior, is a Republican. She is the former President of the Reason Foundation, a libertarian group, and is opposed to recycling, nutritional labeling on food, consumer "right to know" laws, and restrictions on the use of pesticides.

D. Nick Rerras, State Senator in Virginia, is a Republican. He believes that mental illness is caused by demons and, somewhat contradictorily, that "God may be punishing families by giving children mental illnesses." He also claims that "thunder and lightning mean God is mad at you."

John Yoo, Deputy Assistant Attorney General, is a Republican. In January 2002, he sent a 42-page memo to William Haynes II, Chief Legal Counsel for the Pentagon, stating that the Geneva Conventions, the War Crimes Act, and "customary international law" do not apply to the war in Afghanistan. He was seconded by Alberto Gonzales, White House Legal Counsel, who wrote: "In my judgment, this new paradigm renders obsolete Geneva's strict limitations on questioning of enemy prisoners and renders quaint some of its provisions." A few days later, the President suspended all rights for prisoners at Guantanamo Bay.

William Haynes II, the recipient of Yoo's memo, is a Republican. As the Chief Legal Counsel for the Pentagon, he argued that the Defense Department should be exempt from the Migratory Bird Treaty Act, and allowed to test bombs on a Pacific Ocean nesting island. Such bombing, he said, would please bird watchers, because it will make the birds more scarce, and "bird watchers get more enjoyment spotting a rare bird than they do spotting a common one." Haynes has now been nominated by the President for a lifetime appointment as a judge on the US Circuit Court of Appeals.

Republicans like children. John Cornyn, Senator from Texas, speaking in support of the constitutional amendment banning gay marriage, said: "It does not affect your daily life very much if your neighbor marries a box turtle. But that does not mean it is right. Now you must raise your children up in a world where that union of man and box turtle is on the same legal footing as man and wife."

Republicans are optimistic. General Peter Schoomaker, US Army Chief of Staff, says that, following September 11, "there is a huge silver lining in this cloud." He explains: "War is a tremendous focus. . . . Now we have this focusing opportunity, and we have the fact that terrorists have actually attacked our homeland, which it gives it some oomph."

Republicans do not like children. The President has never bothered to appoint a Director of the Office of Children's Health Protection.

Craig Manson, Assistant Secretary of the Interior, is a Republican. In charge of overseeing the Endangered Species

Act, he has refused to add any new species to the list. He said: "If we are saying that the loss of species in and of itself is inherently bad—I don't think we know enough about how the world works to say that."

Elaine Chao, Secretary of Labor, is a Republican. Her department publishes a pamphlet with tips to employers about how to avoid paying overtime wages to workers.

Jack Kahl and his son John Kahl are Republicans and major contributors to the Republican Party. They are, respectively, the former and current chairmen and CEOs of Manco, Inc., a company in Avon, Ohio. (Motto: "If you're not proud of it, don't ship it.") Manco produces 63% of all the duct tape used in the USA. When the Secretary of Homeland Security, Tom Ridge, repeatedly urged Americans to buy plastic sheeting and duct tape to seal their homes from a biological or chemical attack, Manco's sales increased 40% overnight.

Republicans have a sense of history. Sonny Perdue, the Governor of Georgia, celebrated his election victory, and the end of Democratic control, by intoning the words of Martin Luther King: "Free at last, free at last, thank God Almighty, we're free at last!" He gave his speech in front of a large Confederate flag.

Sue Myrick, Congresswoman from North Carolina, is a Republican. As the keynote speaker at a Heritage Foundation conference on "The Role of State and Local Governments in Protecting Our Homeland," she said: "Honest to goodness, [my husband] Ed and I, for years, for 20 years, have been saying, 'You know, look at who runs all the convenience stores across the country.' Every little town you go into, you know?"

Republicans are fighting terrorism. In the village of Prosser, Washington, a 15-year-old drew some anti-war cartoons in a sketchbook for art class; one depicted the President as a devil firing rockets. The art teacher turned the sketchbook over to the principal of the school, who called the local police chief, who alerted the Secret Service, which sent two agents to Prosser to interrogate the boy.

John Hostettler, Congressman from Indiana, is a Republican. He was briefly detained by security at the Louisville, Kentucky, airport, when they found a loaded Glock 9mm automatic pistol in his briefcase. In 2000, when the Violence Against Women Act passed Congress by a vote of 415 to 3, Hostettler was one of the three.

Jeffrey Holmstead, Assistant Administrator for Air and Radiation at the Environmental Protection Agency, is a Republican. A former lawyer for Montrose Chemical, American Electric Power, and various pesticide companies, he served under Bush Sr. on the [Dan] Quayle Council on Competitiveness, devoted to weakening existing environmental, health, and safety regulations. Holmstead is a member of the Citizens for the Environment, an organization that promotes "market solutions" to environmental problems, considers acid rain a myth, and supports the total deregulation of businesses.

Ed Gillespie is Chairman of the Republican National Committee. He accuses gays of "intolerance and bigotry" for "attempting to force the rest of the population to accept alien moral standards."

Al Frink is a Republican. He was appointed to the newly created position of Assistant Secretary of Commerce for Manufacturing and Services, to address the massive loss of jobs to factories overseas. He is the co-owner of Fabrica, a company that makes expensive carpets for the White House and the Saudi royal family. (Motto: "The Rolls-Royce of Carpets.") Although Fabrica has no factories abroad, it has replaced many of its workers with robots because, as Frink's partner explained, you don't have to pay health insurance for robots.

There are American soldiers in Iraq who are Republicans. They follow the instructions to tear out a page from the pamphlet, "A Christian's Duty" (distributed, with military approval, by the In Touch Ministries), and mail it to the White House, pledging that they will pray daily for the Administration. The pamphlet includes a suggested prayer for each day. "Monday" reads: "Pray that the President and his advisers will be strong and courageous to do what is right regardless of critics."

There are men in Indianapolis, Indiana, who are Republicans, but they don't look like ordinary people. At a rally promoting Republican economic policy and its effect on the ordinary person, those standing behind the President were asked to remove their ties and jackets for the cameras.

Republicans are fighting terrorism. Tim Pawlenty, Governor of Minnesota, wants people arrested at anti-war demonstrations—but not at other demonstrations—to pay an additional fine, which will be used for "homeland security expenses."

Republicans do not like children. A little girl asked Richard Riordan, Secretary of Education for the State of California, if he knew that her name, Isis, "meant 'Egyptian goddess.'" "It means stupid, dirty girl," Riordan replied.

Republicans like ice cream, but they do not like the ice cream made by Ben & Jerry's, with its notorious support of progressive causes. So they have created their own brand, Star-Spangled Ice Cream, which has pledged 19% of its profits to conservative organizations. Among its flavors are I Hate the French Vanilla, Gun Nut, Smaller GovernMINT, Iraqi Road, and Choc & Awe.

Jeb Bush, Governor of Florida, is a Republican. He opened the nation's first Christian prison, where inmates spend their days in prayer and Bible study.

Republicans like Hummers. Those who purchase a Hummer H–1 for $50,590 receive a tax deduction of $50,590; those who purchase a H–2 for $111,845 receive a deduction of $107,107. "In my humble opinion," said Rick Schmidt, founder of the International Hummer Owners Group, "the H–2 is an American icon . . . it's a symbol of what we all hold so dearly above all else, the fact we have the freedom of choice, the freedom of happiness, the freedom of adventure and discovery, and the ultimate freedom of expression. Those who deface a Hummer in words or deed deface the American flag and what it stands for."

Republicans like secrets. Asked by a reporter from a newspaper in Apopka, Florida, the White House refused to confirm or deny that it had invited members of the Apopka Little

League team to watch a game of T-ball on the White House lawn.

Republicans have a sense of history. The officials of Taney County, Missouri, refused to hang a "plaque of remembrance" honoring a Taney County resident who died in the World Trade Center on September 11 because he was a Democrat.

Jerry Regier, Director of the Department of Children and Families for the State of Florida, is a Republican. He believes that children should be subject to "manly" discipline, that a "biblical spanking" leading to "temporary and superficial bruises or welts does not constitute child abuse," that women should view working outside the home as "bondage," that Christians should not marry non-Christians, and that "the radical feminist movement has damaged the morale of many women and convinced men to relinquish their biblical authority in the home."

Pete Coors, candidate for Senator from Colorado, is a Republican. Heir to the Coors Beer fortune, he has stated that, if elected, his top priority will be to lower the drinking age.

Republicans have a sense of history. Bill Black, Vice Chairman of the California Republican Party, sent his constituents an article from the Center for Cultural Conservatism, which read: "Given how bad things have gotten in the old USA, it's not hard to believe that history might have taken a better turn. . . . The real damage to race relations in the South came not from slavery, but from Reconstruction, which would not have occurred if the South had won."

Kathy Cox, Superintendent of Schools for the State of Georgia, is a Republican. She wants all textbooks in the state to be changed, so that the word "evolution" is replaced with "biological changes over time."

Jim Bunning, Senator from Kentucky, is a Republican. He gets a laugh at Republican dinners by joking that his opponent in the forthcoming election, Dan Mongiardo, a son of Italian immigrants, looks like one of the sons of Saddam Hussein.

Republicans have a sense of history. The only illustrations in the federal budget, published annually by the Government Printing Office, are normally charts and graphs. This year, it features 27 color photographs of the President. He is seen in front of the Washington Monument and in front of a giant American flag, reading to a small child, hacking a trail through the wilderness, comforting an elderly woman in a wheelchair, and serving an inedible food-styled Thanksgiving turkey to the troops in Iraq.

Republicans do not like almanacs. On Christmas Eve, the FBI sent a bulletin to 18,000 police organizations warning them to watch out—during traffic stops, searches, and other investigations—for anyone carrying an almanac. The bulletin stated that "the practice of researching potential targets is consistent with known methods of al-Qaeda and other terrorist organizations that seek to maximize the likelihood of operational success through careful planning." Kevin Seabrooke, senior editor of the *World Almanac*, may or may not be a Republican. "I don't think anyone would consider us a harmful entity," he said.

Republicans like the *Rush Limbaugh Show* and like having it broadcast to the troops overseas, five days a week, on the official American Forces Radio and Television Service network. When it was suggested that they provide more "balanced" political programming, Sam Johnson, Congressman from Texas, said that it "sounds a little like Communism to me."

Stephen Downs, age 61, is probably not a Republican. He was shopping at the Crossgates Mall in Guilderland, New York, when security guards surrounded him and asked him to leave. Downs was wearing a t-shirt with the words "Give Peace a Chance." He refused to leave and was arrested for trespassing.

My friend, a middle-aged white man, is not a Republican. A photographer on assignment for *National Geographic* in Florida, he was taking pictures of some colorfully painted vans in a parking lot. An hour later he was arrested. An alert citizen, suspecting possible terrorist information-gathering activity, had called the police.

Herbert O. Chadbourne was probably once a Republican. A professor at the evangelical Regent University, he developed a facial tic—the result, he said, of exposure to biological or chemical agents when he was a soldier in the first Gulf War. The university, however, said that the tic was a sign that he was possessed by a demon, having been cursed by God for sinfulness, and fired him.

Jeffrey Kofman, reporter for ABC television, may not be a Republican. When he broadcast a story that morale among American troops in Iraq was weakening, the White House spread the story that not only is Kofman gay, he's a Canadian.

Republicans like technology. Although most programs for low-income housing and job training have been greatly reduced or eliminated, the Department of Labor has created a website for the homeless.

Republicans like methyl bromide, a pesticide that destroys the ozone layer and leads to prostate cancer in farmworkers. The Reagan Administration and 160 nations signed a treaty in 1987 to eliminate methyl bromide by 2005. The use of the pesticide has increased every year of the current Administration, which is seeking a waiver from compliance with the treaty. Claudia A. McMurray, Deputy Assistant Secretary of State for Environment, explained: "Our farmers need this."

Republicans like dog-race gamblers, NASCAR track owners, bow-and-arrow makers, and Oldsmobile dealers. They were among those given $170 billion in tax cuts that were slipped into an obscure bill intended to resolve a minor trade dispute with Europe.

Republicans do not like technology. On September 11, 2001, the FBI computers were still running on MS-DOS, which could only perform single-word searches of their files, and FBI agents did not have e-mail. They are hoping a new system will be in place in 2006.

Lieutenant General William Boykin, Deputy Undersecretary of Defense for Intelligence, formerly in charge of the hunt for Osama bin Laden and currently directing Iraqi prison reform, is a Republican. He regularly appears at revival meetings sponsored by a group called the Faith Force Multiplier, which advocates applying military principles to evangelism. Its manifesto, "Warrior Message," summons "warriors in this spiritual war for souls of this nation and the world." Boykin preaches that "Satan wants to destroy this nation, he wants to destroy us as a nation, and he wants to destroy us as a Christian army," and that Muslims "will only be defeated if we come against them in the name of Jesus." He admits that "George Bush was not elected by a majority of the voters in the US," but adds: "He was appointed by God."

Kelli Arena, Justice Department correspondent for CNN, is presumably a Republican. She reported that "there is some speculation that al-Qaeda believes it has a better chance of winning in Iraq if John Kerry is in the White House."

William "Bucky" Bush, uncle of the President, is a Republican. He is a director of Engineer Support Systems, Inc., which makes military items, such as the Chemical Biological Protected Shelter System (a mobile shed for a WMD attack) or the Field Deployable Environmental Control Unit. Since 2001, the company has had sales to the Pentagon of $300–400 million a year, and the Department of Homeland Security has ordered a fleet of mobile emergency communication centers for use in the event of a domestic bio-chemical attack. He is also a director of Lord Abbett & Co., which owns 8 million shares of Halliburton. Jeb Bush inserted a line in the Florida state budget privatizing elevator inspections. "Bucky" is one of the owners of a company called National Elevator Inspection Services.

Republicans like electronic voting machines. In the 1980s, Bob and Todd Urosevich founded a voting machine company, eventually called American Information Systems (AIS), with money from the Ahmanson family of California. The Ahmansons are Christian Reconstructionists who want to establish a theocracy based on biblical law and under the "dominion" of Christians. They support the death penalty for homosexuals, adulterers, and alcoholics. They are members of the secretive Council for National Policy, which combines remnants of the John Birch Society with apocalyptic Christians and is considered by many to be the driving force of "hard right" ideology. The Ahmansons sold the company to the McCarthy Group, whose Chairman and co-owner was Chuck Hagel. The McCarthy Group bought another voting machine company, Cronus Industries, from the Hunt oil family in Texas, also Christian Reconstructionists, who had supplied the original money for the Council for National Policy. The two voting machine companies were merged and became Election Systems and Software (ES&S), with Hagel as CEO.

Republicans like electronic voting machines. ES&S counts 80% of the vote in the state of Nebraska. In 1992, Hagel resigned from ES&S to run for Senator from Nebraska. His victory was called a "stunning upset" by Nebraska newspapers: African-American districts that had never voted for a Republican voted for Hagel. In 1996, Hagel ran again and received 83% of the vote—3% more than ES&S-tabulated votes and the largest election victory in the history of Nebraska. His Democratic opponent asked for a recount, but the Republican-dominated state legislature had passed a law that only ES&S could recount the votes. Hagel won the recount. No longer Chairman of the McCarthy Group, Hagel had been succeeded by Thomas McCarthy, who was his campaign treasurer.

Republicans like electronic voting machines. When Jeb Bush first ran for Governor of Florida, his first choice for Lieutenant Governor was Sandra Mortham, a lobbyist for ES&S, who was receiving commissions for every county that bought ES&S machines.

Republicans have a sense of history. John LeBoutillier, former Congressman and author of *Harvard Hates America*, wants to build the "Counter Clinton Library," a few minutes walk from the official Clinton Presidential Library in Little Rock, Arkansas. This library will be devoted to the "distortions, slanders, spins, and outright lies" of the Clinton Administration.

The Senate of the State of Texas is controlled by Republicans. They passed an "abortion counseling law" which requires doctors to warn women that abortion might lead to breast cancer, for which there is no medical evidence.

The President's Council of Economic Advisers are Republicans. In order to show an increase in manufacturing jobs, they are considering reclassifying fast-food workers as "manufacturers," since they "manufacture" hamburgers.

Republicans like formaldehyde. In support of changing the regulations on emissions from plywood factories, the White House Office of Management and Budget deleted references to studies by the National Cancer Institute and replaced them with references to studies by the Chemical Industry Institute for Toxicology. The NCI's estimate of the risk of leukemia from exposure to formaldehyde was 10,000 times greater than the estimate by the CIIT.

Republicans are fighting terrorism. When the Governor of Vermont announced that he was suing the federal government to allow senior citizens to import less expensive prescription drugs from Canada, Lester Crawford, Commissioner of the Food and Drug Administration, claimed that al-Qaeda had a plot to poison imported prescription drugs. The Department of Homeland Security admitted "we have no specific information now" about this plot.

George Nethercutt, candidate for Senator from the state of Washington, is a Republican. He attacked the media for reporting American military casualties and ignoring the good news from Iraq, claiming that the reconstruction effort is a "better and more important story than losing a few soldiers every day."

Specialist Sean Baker of the Kentucky National Guard was probably once a Republican, but may no longer be one. Assigned to the military prison in Guantanamo Bay, he volunteered to portray a detainee in a training drill. A five-man "immediate response force" choked and beat him on the steel floor of the 6' x 8' cell, despite his shouting the code word and telling his assailants he was an American soldier. They finally stopped when his orange prison suit was ripped off, revealing a military uniform. Baker spent 48 days in the hospital and still suffers from seizures. Laurie Arellano, a Republican and spokesperson for the Pentagon, said that Baker's hospital stay was "not related to the beating at Guantanamo." A few days later she said this was not true. The incident was taped, but the tape has now been lost.

Bill Nevins may or may not have been a Republican, but it is doubtful he is still one. A teacher at the huge Rio Rancho

High School—with over 3,000 students, the largest in New Mexico—he organized a school poetry club, which held a Poetry Slam. At the reading, a student read a poem criticizing the President and the war in Iraq, in language that was neither violent or obscene. Nevins was immediately fired by the Principal, Gary Tripp, for promoting "disrespectful speech." He then banned the poetry club and all classes in poetry, ordered the student to destroy all of her poetry, and threatened to fire her mother—also a teacher at the school—if the girl did not. At a school assembly a few days later, Tripp read a poem of his own, instructing students who disagreed with him to "shut your faces."

Republicans like sex. Jack Ryan, candidate (now former candidate) for Senator from Illinois, forced his wife (now ex-wife) to visit sadomasochist sex clubs in New York and Paris and insisted she have sex with him there while others watched. He defended himself by calling these "romantic getaways" and noted, "There was no breaking of any laws. There was no breaking of any marriage laws. There was no breaking of the Ten Commandments anywhere." Republicans supported him, because, as columnist Robert Novack said, "Jack Ryan, unlike Bill Clinton, did not commit adultery and did not lie." Ryan's ex-wife is the actress Jeri Ryan who, on the television program *Star Trek*, portrayed a Borg. (Motto: "Resistance is futile.")

Republicans are fighting terrorism. Three weeks before the Democratic Convention, the *New Republic* reported that the White House had been putting pressure on Pakistani intelligence to arrest or assassinate an "HVT" (High Value Terrorist) in time for the Convention. On the day of Kerry's speech, they announced the arrest of one Muhammad Naeem Noor Khan.

A few days later, New York City, Washington, DC, and Newark, New Jersey, were put on even more heightened Terror Alert after it was revealed that Khan's computer disks contained surveillance and blueprints of five financial buildings. Tom Ridge, Secretary of Homeland Security, insisting that this Terror Alert was indeed more serious and specific than all the previous Terror Alerts, concluded his press conference by saying: "We must understand that the kind of information available to us today is the result of the President's leadership in the war against terror."

Republicans are fighting terrorism. The day after Ridge's announcement, it was revealed that the al-Qaeda documents had been created in 2000 and 2001, before September 11. The day after that, it was admitted that there were no blueprints. A few days later, British intelligence officials expressed their rage that Khan not only had been arrested, but had been named. Khan may have been the only double agent within al-Qaeda, and had supplied them with information leading to dozens of arrests of al-Qaeda members.

Joe Lieberman, Senator from Connecticut and former Vice Presidential candidate, is supposedly not a Republican. He said: "I don't think anybody who has any fairness or is in their right mind would think the President or the Secretary of Homeland Security would raise an alert level and scare people for political reasons."

Republicans like meat, and like their meat regulated by people from the meat industry. At the US Department of Agriculture (USDA), Elizabeth Johnson, Senior Advisor on Food and Nutrition, is formerly Associate Director for Food

Policy, National Cattlemen's Beef Association. James Moseley, Deputy Secretary of Agriculture, is formerly Managing Partner, Infinity Pork. Dale Moore, Chief of Staff, is formerly Executive Director for Legislative Affairs, National Cattlemen's Beef Association. Dr. Eric Hentges, Director, Center for Nutrition Policy and Promotion, is formerly Vice President, the National Pork Board. Dr. Charles "Chuck" Lambert, Deputy Undersecretary for Marketing and Regulatory Programs, is formerly Chief Economist, National Cattlemen's Beef Association. Donna Reifschneider, Administrator for Grain Inspection, Packers and Stockyards Administration, is formerly President, National Pork Producers Council. Mary Kirtley Waters, Assistant Secretary for Congressional Relations, is formerly Senior Director, ConAgra Foods. Scott Charbo, Chief Information Officer, is formerly President, mPower3, a subsidiary of ConAgra Foods. The USDA prohibited Creekstone Farms Premium Beef, a company in Kansas, from testing all its cattle for mad cow disease, for it would cause undue alarm among consumers and pressure the other beef producers to similarly test their stock.

Joe Brown, Chairman of the Memphis, Tennessee, City Council, is a Republican. When a group of seven Iraqi "civic and community leaders" on a State Department tour of the US visited Memphis, he refused to allow them to enter the City Hall: "We don't know exactly what's going on. Who knows about the delegation, and has the FBI been informed? We must secure and protect all the employees in that building." Brown told the group's host he would "evacuate the building and bring in the bomb squads" if the group attempted to come in.

Republicans like Freedom fries (formerly known as French fries). At the request of the frozen Freedom fry (formerly known as French fry) industry, the USDA changed the classification of frozen Freedom fries (formerly known as French fries) to "fresh vegetable," so that the food could be listed in the Department's promotion of a healthy diet.

Republicans do not like sex. Robert F. McDonnell, Chairman of the House Courts of Justice Committee for the State of Virginia, said that "engaging in anal or oral sex might disqualify a person from being a judge." Republicans like sex. A few days later, McDonnell's campaign manager, Robin Vanderwell, was arrested for soliciting a young boy over the internet.

Ralph Reed is a Republican. When he was the director of the Christian Coalition, he campaigned against gambling, calling it a "cancer on the American body politic" that is "stealing food from the mouths of children." He is now the lobbyist for a large casino.

Anna Perez, former Counselor for Communications to Condoleezza Rice and former Press Secretary for Barbara Bush, is a Republican. NBC appointed her Executive Vice President for Communications. "I love the television business," she said, although "I have no expertise in it."

Paul O'Neill is a Republican. When he was Secretary of the Treasury, he recommended that corporations pay no taxes at all. As it is, only 60% of corporations currently pay federal taxes.

Michael Skupkin, founder of a religious software company and leader of the Presidential Prayer Team, is a Republican. He was urged to run for Senator from Michigan, but eventually refused. Skupkin had become famous on the television program, *Survivor 2*, for catching and slaughtering a wild boar with his bare hands, and then painting his face with its blood. The Presidential Prayer Team is an independent organization with millions of participants, who are given daily instructions, such as: "Pray for the President as he meets with Singaporean Prime Minister Goh Chok Ton on May 6. The two leaders will discuss strengthening our bilateral relations as well as the US-Singapore Free Trade Agreement."

Mark Rey, former Vice President of the American Forest and Paper Association, former Vice President of the National Forest Products Association, former Executive Director of the American Forest Resource Alliance, a coalition of 350 timber corporations, is a Republican. As the Under Secretary for Natural Resources and the Environment, he now oversees the US Forest Service, and is responsible for the management of 155 national forests, 19 national grasslands, and 15 land utilization projects on 192,000,000 acres of publicly owned lands in 44 states. He is the author of the "Salvage Rider," which suspended all environmental laws in the national forests, and which was called by the *New York Times* "the worst piece of conservation legislation ever written."

Republicans like electronic voting machines. 8 million people—8% of the voters—vote on machines made by Diebold Inc., whose CEO is Wally O'Dell. In 2000 O'Dell was Chairman of the Ohio Bush for President Committee. In 2004 he has said that he is "committed to helping Ohio deliver its electoral votes to the President." Bob Urosevich, co-founder of AIS, is now Director of Diebold Election Systems. (His brother remains at ES&S.)

Republicans support education. This year the President has proposed new education initiatives: $40 million to help math and science professionals become teachers, $52 million to create more Advanced Placement courses in high school, $100 million for reading for middle and high schoolers who still have trouble reading, and $270 million for sexual abstinence classes.

Republicans support legislation with cheerful names: Healthy Forests, Clean Skies, Climate Leaders, No Child Left Behind, KidCare. Healthy Forests opens up Sequoia National Park and other parks and national wilderness areas to logging and more roads for loggers. Clean Skies allows 68% more nitrogen oxide, 125% more sulfur dioxide, and 420% more mercury air pollution than the Clean Air law it replaces. Climate Leaders is a plan for businesses to voluntarily reduce their greenhouse gas emissions; of the many thousands of potential Leaders, only 14 have volunteered. No Child Left Behind cuts most school programs in favor of standardized testing. KidCare, a Jeb Bush initiative in the state of Florida, resulted in 167,500 children losing their medical insurance.

Jerry Thacker, marketing consultant and former member of the Presidential Advisory Commission on AIDS and HIV, is a Republican. He has called AIDS the "gay plague," describes homosexuality as a "deathstyle," and states that only "Christ can rescue the homosexual."

The Rev. Scott Breedlove, pastor of the Jesus Church of Cedar Rapids, Iowa, is probably a Republican. His plans for a large outdoor book-burning were thwarted by officials of the Cedar Rapids Fire Department. A city fire inspector suggested shredding the books, but Breedlove said that didn't seem very biblical.

Pat Tillman was probably a Republican. After September 11, he gave up a multimillion-dollar contract as a professional football player to join the Army Rangers in Afghanistan, where he died in combat. As the only soldier with some previous national recognition, he was on the verge of media canonization when it was revealed that he had been killed by American troops in a "friendly fire" incident.

Zell Miller, Senator from Georgia, might as well be a Republican. He is a Democrat who campaigns for the President and speaks at Republican events. The torture at Abu Ghraib prison reminded him of his high school gym: "The two times I think I have been most humiliated in my life was standing in a big room, naked as a jaybird with about fifty others and they were checking us out, now that was humiliating. It was humiliating showering with sixty others in a public shower. It didn't kill us did it? No one ever died from humiliation."

Republicans are fighting terrorism. Police and intelligence authorities are now examining immigration files and lists of voter registration, driver's licences, university enrollment, library withdrawals, airplane reservations, credit card purchases, birth certificates, and Social Security numbers in the attempt to uncover terrorist links. They have, however, been expressly forbidden by Attorney General Ashcroft from looking at the lists of background checks for gun purchasers.

Republicans are fighting terrorism, but it is sometimes difficult to tell who is a terrorist and who is a Republican. Attorney General John Ashcroft has warned that al-Qaeda operatives in the United States are very likely to be "European-looking," in their late twenties or early thirties, traveling with their families, and speaking English.

Republicans like large bombs. Having already developed the Massive Ordnance Air Blast (MOAB), a 21,000-pound bomb, they are now working on MOP, the Massive Ordnance Penetrator, which weighs 30,000 pounds.

Rick Perry, Governor of Texas, is a Republican. He does not believe that the wealthy should pay for the education of the poor, so he has proposed reducing property taxes and replacing them with larger taxes on cigarettes and alcohol, and a $5 tax every time a patron enters a topless bar.

John Graham, former CEO of Strat@comm, a public relations and lobbying firm for the automobile industry, and founder of the Sports Utility Vehicle Owners of America, is a Republican. As the Administrator in Charge of Regulations for the National Highway Traffic Safety Administration, he has introduced greatly inferior standards for automobile tires.

Judge John Leon Holmes, appointed by the President to a lifetime seat on the Federal District Court, is a Republican. He supports a constitutional amendment banning abortion, has compared pro-choice advocates to Nazis and abortion to slavery, and has written that "concern for rape victims is a red herring because conceptions from rape occur with approximately the same frequency as snowfall in Miami." Confronted with statistics showing that some 30,000 American women become pregnant each year from rape or incest, Jeff Sessions, Senator from Alabama and a Republican, defended Holmes by saying that he was merely using "a literary device called 'exaggeration' for effect."

Josh Llano, Southern Baptist Army chaplain in Iraq, is a Republican. At the Army V Corps camp in the desert near Najaf, where water is in short supply and washing rare, he was given a 500-gallon pool to use for baptisms. Soldiers are agreeing to sit through the three-hour ceremony in order to get a bath.

Republicans are fighting terrorism. Rick Santorum, Senator from Pennsylvania, in support of the constitutional amendment banning gay marriage, said: "I would argue that the future of our country hangs in the balance because the future of marriage hangs in the balance. Isn't that the ultimate homeland security, standing up and defending marriage?"

Republicans are fighting terrorism. In October 2001, Ansar Mahmood, a pizza delivery man and legal immigrant in Hudson, New York, went to the banks of the Hudson River to take some photographs of the beautiful scenery to send to his village in Pakistan. What he did not know was that he was standing near a water treatment plant and that there was a general hysteria about terrorists poisoning the water supply. Mahmood is still in jail.

James Hart, candidate for Congress from Tennessee, is a Republican. An ardent supporter of eugenics, he believes that Africans and African-Americans have an average IQ of 75, and that if interracial marriage had been allowed in the past, the electric light, the automobile, and the airplane would never have been invented.

Allan Fitzsimmons, Fuels Coordinator at the Department of Interior and in charge of implementing the Healthy Forests initiative, is a Republican. Although he has no background in forest management, he has written articles questioning the existence of ecosystems, calling them a "mental construct." He has accused religious organizations that promote protecting the environment of succumbing to idolatry.

Republicans do not like children. The Food and Drug Administration has eliminated laws requiring separate testing for drugs that are prescribed for children as well as adults.

Republicans like to help impoverished nations. The Administration has proposed that these countries generate income by allowing hunters to kill elephants and other "trophy" animals, and wildlife traders and the pet industry to capture rare birds. It has also proposed that the importation of ivory tusks, skins, and antlers be made legal again.

Republicans like electronic voting machines. It was a surprise when Max Cleland, a popular Democratic Senator from Georgia, lost his bid for re-election. Some attributed the defeat to Republican television advertisements juxtaposing Cleland with Osama bin Laden, questioning the Senator's patriotism, even though Cleland had lost both legs and an arm in the Vietnam War. This was the first election in which all votes in Georgia were cast on electronic voting machines. The machines were manufactured by Diebold.

Republicans do not like international treaties.

Randall Tobias, global coordinator for AIDS, is a Republican. After two years, only 2% of the $18 billion allotted to fight AIDS has been spent. One third of it, by law, must be used for "abstinence education." Much of the rest will be spent on drugs. Tobias decides whether the Administration will purchase generic drugs or name-brand drugs, which are three to five times as expensive. Tobias is the former CEO of the pharmaceutical corporation Eli Lilly, which has donated at least $1.5 million to Republicans since 2000.

William G. Myers, recently appointed to a lifetime seat on the Court of Appeals, is a Republican. Evidently a classical scholar, he referred to the California Desert Protection Act, which created Joshua Tree National Park, Death Valley National Park, and the Mojave National Preserve, as "an example of legislative hubris."

Republicans like electronic voting machines. The State of Maryland is worried about possible fraud in its machines, so it has hired the Science Applications International Corporation (SAIC) to oversee elections. The former CEO of SAIC and current Chairman of its VoteHere division is Admiral Bill Owens, former military aide to Dick Cheney.

Republicans do not like the cactus pygmy owl, although there are only thirty left, Puget Sound orcas, Florida manatees, Florida panthers, or the Kemp's ridley turtle.

Cindy Jacobs is a Republican. She is the founder of the Generals of Intercession, an organization devoted to "winning nations for Christ" through a "military-style prayer strategy." In 2002, God told her that the US would invade Iraq, and she convened an "international gathering of Generals" in Washington, D.C. "Each of us felt in our hearts that God wants to humble the spirit of Islam and its god, Allah, and that God is leading President Bush." At the meeting, according to Jacobs, one of the Generals said "she had been studying Jeremiah 50:2, which says, 'Declare among the nations, Proclaim, and set up a standard; Proclaim—do not conceal it—Say, Babylon is taken, Bel is shamed.' Some Bible translations say 'confounded' rather than 'shamed.' As she looked up the word 'confounded' in her lexicon, she found that the word in Hebrew is 'Bush'! We were amazed at that!"

Mickey Mouse is a Republican. 7.3 million shares of Disney are owned by the Florida state pension fund, which is controlled by Jeb Bush. Disney has an agreement with the state granting them complete control, "free from government oversight," of over 40,000 acres. In the days following September 11, the President urged the country to "Go down to Disney World in Florida. Take your families and enjoy life." Disney refused to allow its Miramax division to distribute the Michael Moore film *Fahrenheit 9/11*.

Republicans are fighting terrorism, but the one genuine terrorist captured, accidentally, on American soil has never been mentioned in the 2,295 press releases issued by John Ashcroft and the Office of the Attorney General. William Krar of Noonday, Texas, mailed a package containing false UN credentials, Defense Intelligence Agency identification cards, phony birth certificates, and forged federal concealed weapons permits to a fellow terrorist. The Post Office delivered it to the wrong address, and the recipient notified the FBI. At Krar's home they found fully automatic machine guns, remote-controlled explosive devices disguised as briefcases, 60 pipe bombs, 500,000 rounds of ammunition, and enough pure sodium cyanide, as the FBI said, "to kill everyone inside a 30,000 square-foot building." Krar, however, is a White Supremacist, and not a Muslim.

Republicans do not like elections. After the Presidential election of 2000, Congress approved $4 billion to help states improve their voting systems for the 2004 election. Very little of the money has been distributed. Congress also created the Election Assistance Commission to oversee these improvements. For years, the White House delayed appointing any members or providing any of the funds appropriated. In 2004, it named DeForest "Buster" Soaries Jr., a New Jersey minister, as Director of the Commission. His first act was to ask for emergency legislation from Congress giving the Commission the authority to cancel the elections in the event of a terrorist attack.

God is a Republican. Speaking to a group of Amish farmers, the President told them: "God speaks through me."

Republicans have a sense of history. Mitch McConnell, Senator from Kentucky, wants to replace Alexander Hamilton on the $10 bill with Ronald Reagan. Dana Rohrabacher, Congressman from California, wants to replace Andrew Jackson on the $20 bill with Ronald Reagan. Jeff Miller, Congressman from Florida, wants to replace John Kennedy on the 50-cent piece with Ronald Reagan. Mark Souder, Congressman from Indiana, wants to replace Franklin Roosevelt on the dime with Ronald Reagan. Bill Frist, Senate Majority Leader, wants to rename the Pentagon as the Ronald Reagan National Defense Building. Grover Norquist of the Leave Us Alone Coalition (whose weekly meetings are attended by representatives of the President and Vice President) and Director of the Ronald Reagan Legacy Project, wants to put a monument to Ronald Reagan in every one of the 3,000 counties in the United States. Matt Salmon, Congressman from Arizona, wants Ronald Reagan's head carved on Mount Rushmore.

George W. Bush, President of the United States, is a Republican. To demonstrate personal sacrifice and his determination to win the War on Terror, he gave up desserts and candy a few days before he announced the invasion of Iraq.

FREEDOM IS ON THE MARCH

[23 October 2004]

Among the things the second term of the Bush junta will bring is the New Freedom Initiative. This is a proposal, barely reported in the press, to give all Americans—beginning with schoolchildren—a standardized test for mental illness. Those who flunk the test will be issued medication, and those who do not want to take their medication will be urged to have it implanted under their skin. Needless to say, the New Freedom Commission, appointed by the President, is composed almost entirely of executives, lawyers, and lobbyists for pharmaceutical corporations.

The question is: Will anyone pass the test? Half of America is clearly deranged, and it has driven the other half mad.

The President openly declares that God speaks through him. The Republicans are making television advertisements featuring the actor who played Jesus in Mel Gibson's *The Passion of the Christ*, while sending out pamphlets that warn that if Kerry is elected he will ban the Bible. Catholic bishops have decreed that voting for Kerry is a sin (mortal or venial?) that must be confessed before one can take communion. The one piece of scientific research actively promoted by the government is investigating whether having others pray for you can cure cancer. (The National Institute of Health has explained that this is "imperative" because poor people have limited access to normal health care.) At the official gift shop in Grand Canyon National Park, they sell a book that states that this so-called natural wonder sprang fully formed in the six days of Creation. We already know that the current United States government does not believe in global warming or the hazards of pollution; now we know it doesn't believe in erosion either.

The polls are evidence that the country is suffering a collective head injury. On any given issue—the economy, the war in Iraq, health care—the majority perceive that the situation is bad and the President has handled it badly. Yet these same people, in these same polls, also say they'll be voting for Bush. Like battered wives—realizing yet denying what is happening, still making excuses for their men—the voters are ruled by fear and intimidation and the threat of worse to come. They've been beaten up by the phantom of terrorism.

Every few weeks we're bludgeoned by warnings that terrorists may strike in a matter of days. Incited by the Department of Homeland Security, millions have bought duct tape and plastic sheeting to protect their homes from biological and chemical attack, and have amassed caches of canned food and bottled water. To ensure that everyone everywhere stays afraid, 10,000 FBI agents have been sent to small towns to talk to local police chiefs about what they can do to fight terrorism. After the massacre at Beslan, school principals received letters from the Department of Education instructing them to beware of strangers. The Vice President intones that if Kerry is elected, terrorists will be exploding nuclear bombs in the cities. (And, to anticipate all possibilities, also warns that terrorists may set off bombs before the election to influence the vote. . . but we're not going to let them tell Americans who to vote for, are we?)

America doesn't feel like America anymore. Fear has infected even the most common transactions of daily life. It is not only visitors to the US who are treated as criminals, with fingerprints and photographs and retinal scans. Anyone entering any anonymous office building must now go through security clearances worthy of an audience with Donald Rumsfeld. At provincial airports, there are frequent announcements in that assuring, disembodied voice of science-fiction films: "The Department of Homeland Security advises that the Terror Alert is now . . . Code Orange." Fear of flying has been replaced by fear of checking in. Nearly every day there are stories of people arrested or detained for innocuous activities, like snapping a photo of a friend in the subway or wearing an anti-war button while shopping in the mall. Worst of all, the whole country has acquiesced to the myth of terrorist omnipotence. Even those who laugh at the color-coded Alerts and other excesses of the anti-terror apparatus do not question the need for the apparatus itself. The Department of Homeland Security, after all, was a Democratic proposal first rejected by Bush.

Common sense has retreated to the monasteries of a few websites. It is considered delusional to suggest that international terrorism is nothing more than a criminal activity performed by a handful of people, that al-Qaeda and similar groups are the Weather Underground, the Red Brigade, the Baader-Meinhof Gang, with more sophisticated techniques and more powerful weapons, operating in the age of 24-hour television news. They are not an army. They are not waging a war. They are tiny groups perpetrating isolated acts of violence.

There's no question they are dangerous individuals, but—without demeaning the indelible trauma of 9/11 or the Madrid bombings—the danger they pose must be seen with some kind of dispassionate perspective. A terrorist attack is a rare and sudden disaster, the manmade equivalent of an earthquake or flood. More people die in the US every year from choking on food than died in the Twin Towers. About 35,000 die annually from gunshot wounds. (While Bush lifts the ban on assault weapons, and both Bush and Kerry promote gun ownership, a captured al-Qaeda manual recommends traveling to the US to buy weapons.) About 45,000 die in car crashes—while the Bush administration lowers automobile safety standards to increase the profits of the auto industry, major donors to his campaign. Millions, of course, die from diseases, and one can only imagine if the billions spent on useless elephantine bureaucracies like the Department of Homeland Security had gone to hospitals and research. If the goal were genuinely to protect lives, fighting terrorism would be a serious matter for police and intelligence agencies, and a small project of a nation's well-being.

Compare, for a moment, Spain. After the Madrid bombings, the police, in a few days, arrested those responsible. (After 9/11, the US rounded up more than 5,000 people—many of whom are still in jail and not a single one of whom has been proven to have any connection to any form of terrorist activity.) They did not carpet-bomb Morocco. They are quietly increasing police surveillance without Terror Alert national panics and with little or no interruption of daily life. And, geographically, demographically, and historically (the fundamentalist dream of recuperating al-Andalus), there is a much greater possibility of another terrorist attack in Spain than in the US.

But of course the current "war on terrorism" is not about saving lives at all; it's about keeping power in the hands of a tiny cell of ideologues. In the manner of all totalitarian societies, the Bush junta, with a happily compliant mass media, has wildly exaggerated the power of the Enemy. This has allowed them to wage a war in Iraq they began planning long before 9/11 and to plot further invasions, to suspend

Constitutional rights and disdain international law, to enrich their friends and ignore the opinions of most of the world. Many Americans who dislike Bush will still vote for him in November because the marketing campaign has made him appear the resolute "wartime" Commander-in-Chief who will keep the nation "safe." It has become futile to try to argue that this war on terror doesn't exist, and that the actual war in Iraq has nothing to do with the safety of Americans at home, and that abroad it has killed or maimed more Americans than 9/11. It remains to be seen what price the country, and the world, will pay for this fantasy.

An unnamed "senior adviser" to Bush recently told the journalist Ron Suskind that people like Suskind were members of "what we call the reality-based community": those who "believe that solutions emerge from [the] judicious study of discernible reality." However, he explained, "That's not the way the world really works anymore. We're an empire now, and when we act, we create our own reality. And while you're studying that reality . . . we'll act again, creating other new realities, which you can study too, and that's how things will sort out. We're history's actors, and you, all of you, will be left to just study what we do."

   This may well be the clearest expression yet of the Bush Doctrine. To become enraged by particulars—the daily slaughter in Iraq, the prison torture, the worst economy since the Great Depression, the banana republic tricks and slanders of the electoral campaign—is to miss the point. We are no longer in "discernible reality." In the second term, the only choice will be to line up for your medication and enjoy the New Freedom. As Bush now says in every speech, "Freedom is on the march."

WHAT I HEARD ABOUT IRAQ

[12 January 2005]

In 1992, a year after the first Gulf War, I heard Dick Cheney, then Secretary of Defense, say that the US had been wise not to invade Baghdad and get "bogged down in the problems of trying to take over and govern Iraq." I heard him say: "The question in my mind is: How many additional American casualties is Saddam worth? And the answer is: Not very damned many."

In February 2001, I heard Colin Powell say that Saddam Hussein "has not developed any significant capability with respect to weapons of mass destruction. He is unable to project conventional power against his neighbors."

That same month, I heard that a CIA report stated: "We do not have any direct evidence that Iraq has used the period since Desert Fox to reconstitute its weapons of mass destruction programs."

In July 2001, I heard Condoleezza Rice say: "We are able to keep his arms from him. His military forces have not been rebuilt."

On September 11, 2001, six hours after the attacks, I heard that Donald Rumsfeld said that it might be an opportunity to "hit" Iraq. I heard that he said: "Go massive. Sweep it all up. Things related and not."

I heard that Condoleezza Rice asked: "How do you capitalize on these opportunities?"

I heard that on September 17 the President signed a document marked "TOP SECRET" that directed the Pentagon to begin planning for the invasion and that, some months later, he secretly and illegally diverted $700 million approved by Congress for operations in Afghanistan into preparing for the new battlefront.

In February 2002, I heard that an unnamed "senior military commander" said: "We are moving military and intelligence personnel and resources out of Afghanistan to get ready for a future war in Iraq."

I heard the President say that Iraq is "a threat of unique urgency," and that there is "no doubt the Iraqi regime continues to possess the most lethal weapons ever devised."

I heard the Vice President say: "Simply stated, there is no doubt that Saddam Hussein now has weapons of mass destruction."

I heard the President tell Congress, "The danger to our country is grave. The danger to our country is growing. The regime is seeking a nuclear bomb, and with fissile material, could build one within a year."

I heard him say: "The dangers we face will only worsen from month to month and from year to year. To ignore these threats is to encourage them. And when they have fully materialized it may be too late to protect ourselves and our friends and our allies. By then the Iraqi dictator would have the means to terrorize and dominate the region. Each passing day could be the one on which the Iraqi regime gives anthrax or VX—nerve gas—or some day a nuclear weapon to a terrorist ally."

I heard the President, in the State of the Union address, say that Iraq was hiding 25,000 liters of anthrax, 38,000 liters of botulinum toxin, and 500 tons of sarin, mustard, and nerve gas.

I heard the President say that Iraq had attempted to purchase uranium—later specified as "yellowcake" uranium oxide from Niger—and thousands of aluminum tubes "suitable for nuclear weapons production."

I heard the Vice President say: "We know that he's been absolutely devoted to trying to acquire nuclear weapons, and we believe he has, in fact, reconstituted nuclear weapons."

I heard the President say: "Imagine those 19 hijackers with other weapons and other plans—this time armed by Saddam Hussein. It would take one vial, one canister, one crate slipped into this country to bring a day of horror like none we have ever known."

I heard Donald Rumsfeld say: "Some have argued that the nuclear threat from Iraq is not imminent. I would not be so certain."

I heard the President say: "America must not ignore the threat gathering against us. Facing clear evidence of peril, we cannot wait for the final proof—the smoking gun—that could come in the form of a mushroom cloud."

I heard Condoleezza Rice say: "We don't want the 'smoking gun' to be a mushroom cloud."

I heard the American Ambassador to the European Union tell the Europeans: "You had Hitler in Europe and no one really did anything about him. The same type of person is in Baghdad."

I heard Colin Powell at the United Nations say: "They can produce enough dry biological agent in a single month to kill thousands upon thousands of people. Saddam Hussein has never accounted for vast amounts of chemical weaponry: 550 artillery shells with mustard gas, 30,000 empty munitions, and enough precursors to increase his stockpile to as much as 500 tons of chemical agents. Our conservative estimate is that Iraq today has a stockpile of between 100 and 500 tons of chemical-weapons agent. Even the low end of 100 tons of agent would enable Saddam Hussein to cause mass casualties across more than 100 square miles of territory, an area nearly five times the size of Manhattan."

I heard him say: "Every statement I make today is backed up by sources, solid sources. These are not assertions. What we're giving you are facts and conclusions based on solid intelligence."

I heard the President say that "Iraq has a growing fleet of manned and unmanned aerial vehicles that could be used to disperse chemical or biological weapons across broad areas." I heard him say that Iraq "could launch a biological or chemical attack in as little as 45 minutes after the order is given."

I heard Tony Blair say: "We are asked to accept Saddam decided to destroy those weapons. I say that such a claim is palpably absurd."

I heard the President say: "We know that Iraq and al-Qaeda have had high-level contacts that go back a decade. We've learned that Iraq has trained al-Qaeda members in bomb-making and poisons and deadly gases. Alliance with terrorists could allow the Iraq regime to attack America without leaving any fingerprints."

I heard the Vice President say: "There's overwhelming evidence there was a connection between al-Qaeda and the Iraqi government. I am very confident there was an established relationship there."

I heard Colin Powell say: "Iraqi officials deny accusations of ties with al-Qaeda. These denials are simply not credible."

I heard Condoleezza Rice say: "There clearly are contacts between al-Qaeda and Saddam Hussein that can be documented."

I heard the President say: "You can't distinguish between al-Qaeda and Saddam."

I heard Donald Rumsfeld say: "Imagine a September eleventh with weapons of mass destruction. It's not three thousand— it's tens of thousands of innocent men, women, and children."

I heard Colin Powell tell the Senate that "a moment of truth is coming": "This is not just an academic exercise or the United States being in a fit of pique. We're talking about real weapons. We're talking about anthrax. We're talking about botulinum toxin. We're talking about nuclear weapons programs."

I heard Donald Rumsfeld say: "No terrorist state poses a greater or more immediate threat to the security of our people."

I heard the President, "bristling with irritation," say: "This business about time, how much time do we need to see clearly that he's not disarming? He is delaying. He is deceiving. He is asking for time. He's playing hide-and-seek with inspectors. One thing for sure is, he's not disarming. Surely our friends have learned lessons from the past. This looks like a rerun of a bad movie and I'm not interested in watching it."

I heard that, a few days before authorizing the invasion of Iraq, the Senate was told, in a classified briefing by the Pentagon, that Iraq could launch anthrax and other biological and chemical weapons against the Eastern seaboard of the United States using unmanned aerial "drones."

I heard Donald Rumsfeld say he would present no specific evidence of Iraqi weapons of mass destruction because it might jeopardize the military mission by revealing to Baghdad what the United States knows.

◆ ◆ ◆

I heard the Pentagon spokesman call the military plan "A-Day," or "Shock and Awe." Three or four hundred Cruise missiles launched every day, until "there will not be a safe place in Baghdad," until "you have this simultaneous effect, rather like the nuclear weapons at Hiroshima, not taking days or weeks but in minutes." I heard the spokesman say: "You're sitting in Baghdad and all of a sudden you're the general and thirty of your division headquarters have been wiped out. You also take the city down. By that I mean you get rid of their power, water. In 2, 3, 4, 5 days they are physically, emotionally and psychologically exhausted." I heard him say: "The sheer size of this has never been seen before, never contemplated."

I heard Major General Charles Swannack promise that his troops were going to "use a sledgehammer to smash a walnut."

I heard the Pentagon spokesman say: "This is not going to be your father's Persian Gulf War."

I heard that Saddam's strategy against the American invasion would be to blow up dams, bridges, and the oil fields; and to cut off food supplies to the south, so that the Americans would suddenly have to feed millions of desperate civilians. I heard that Baghdad would be encircled by two rings of the elite Republican Guard, in fighting positions already stocked with weapons and supplies, and equipped with chemical protective gear against the poison gas or germ weapons they would be using against the American troops.

I heard Vice Admiral Lowell Jacoby tell Congress that Saddam would "employ a 'scorched earth' strategy, destroying food, transportation, energy and other infrastructures, attempting to create a humanitarian disaster," and that he would blame it all on the Americans.

I heard that Iraq would fire its long-range Scud missiles, equipped with chemical or biological warheads, at Israel, to "portray the war as a battle with an American-Israeli coalition and build support in the Arab world."

I heard that Saddam had elaborate and labyrinthine underground bunkers for his protection, and that it might be necessary to employ B–61 Mod 11 nuclear "bunker-buster" bombs to destroy them.

I heard the Vice President say that the war would be over in "weeks rather than months."

I heard Donald Rumsfeld say: "It could last six days, six weeks. I doubt six months."

I heard Donald Rumsfeld say there was "no question" that American troops would be "welcomed": "Go back to Afghanistan, the people were in the streets playing music, cheering, flying kites, and doing all the things that the Taliban and the al-Qaeda would not let them do."

I heard the Vice President say: "The Middle East expert Professor Fouad Ajami predicts that after liberation the streets in Basra and Baghdad are 'sure to erupt in joy . . .' Extremists in the region would have to rethink their strategy of Jihad. Moderates throughout the region would take heart. And our ability to advance the Israeli-Palestinian peace process would be enhanced."

I heard the Vice President say: "I really do believe we will be greeted as liberators."

I heard Tariq Aziz, the Iraqi Foreign Minister say: "American soldiers will not be received by flowers. They will be received by bullets."

I heard that the President told the television evangelist Pat Robertson: "Oh, we're not going to have any casualties."

I heard the President say that he had not consulted with his father about the coming war: "You know he is the wrong father to appeal to in terms of strength. There is a higher father I appeal to."

I heard the Prime Minister of the Solomon Islands express surprise that his was one of the nations enlisted in the Coalition of the Willing: "I was completely unaware of it."

I heard the President tell the Iraqi people, on the night before the invasion began: "If we must begin a military campaign, it will be directed against the lawless men who rule your country and not against you. As our Coalition takes away their power we will deliver the food and medicine you need. We will tear down the apparatus of terror. And we will help you build a new Iraq that is prosperous and free. In a free Iraq there will be no more wars of aggression against your neighbors, no more poison factories, no more executions of dissidents, no more torture chambers and rape rooms. The tyrant will soon be gone. The day of your liberation is near."

I heard him tell the Iraqi people: "We will not relent until your country is free."

◆ ◆ ◆

I heard the Vice President say: "By any standard of even the most dazzling charges in military history, the Germans in the Ardennes in the spring of 1940 or Patton's romp in July of 1944, the present race to Baghdad is unprecedented in its speed and daring and in the lightness of casualties."

I heard Colonel David Hackworth say: "Hey diddle diddle, it's straight up the middle!"

I heard the Pentagon spokesman say that 95% of the Iraqi casualties were "military-age males."

I heard an official from the Red Crescent say: "On one stretch of highway alone, there were more than 50 civilian cars, each with four or five people incinerated inside, that sat in the sun for 10 or 15 days before they were buried nearby by volunteers. That is what there will be for their relatives to come and find. War is bad, but its remnants are worse."

I heard the director of a hospital in Baghdad say: "The whole hospital is an emergency room. The nature of the injuries is so severe—one body without a head, someone else with their abdomen ripped open." I heard him say: "Human beings are so frail in the face of these weapons of war."

I heard an American soldier say: "There's a picture of the World Trade Center hanging up by my bed and I keep one in my Kevlar [flak jacket]. Every time I feel sorry for these people I look at that. I think, 'They hit us at home and now it's our turn.'"

I heard about Hashim, a fat, "painfully shy" 15-year-old, who liked to sit for hours by the river with his birdcage, and who was shot by the 4th Infantry Division in a raid on his village. Asked about the details of the boy's death, the Division Commander said: "That person was probably in the wrong place at the wrong time."

I heard an American soldier say: "We get rocks thrown at us by kids. You wanna turn around and shoot one of the little fuckers, but you know you can't do that."

I heard the Pentagon spokesman say that the US did not count civilian casualties: "Our efforts focus on destroying the enemy's capabilities, so we never target civilians and have no reason to try to count such unintended deaths." I heard him say that, in any event, it would be impossible, because the Iraqi paramilitaries were fighting in civilian clothes, the military was using civilian human shields, and many of the civilian deaths were the result of Iraqi "unaimed anti-aircraft fire falling back to earth."

I heard an American soldier say: "The worst thing is to shoot one of them, then go help him," as regulations require. "Shit, I didn't help any of them. I wouldn't help the fuckers. There were some you let die. And there were some you double-tapped. Once you'd reached the objective, and once you'd shot them and you're moving through, anything there, you shoot again. You didn't want any prisoners of war."

I heard Anmar Uday, the doctor who had cared for Private Jessica Lynch, say: "We heard the helicopters. We were surprised. Why do this? There was no military. There were no soldiers in the hospitals. It was like a Hollywood film. They cried 'Go, go, go,' with guns and flares and the sound of explosions. They made a show—an action movie like Sylvester Stallone or Jackie Chan, with jumping and shouting, breaking down doors. All the time with cameras rolling."

I heard Private Jessica Lynch say: "They used me as a way to symbolize all this stuff. It hurt in a way that people would make up stories that they had no truth about." I heard her say, about the stories that she had bravely fought off her captors, and suffered bullet and stab wounds: "I'm not about to take credit for something I didn't do." I heard her say, about her dramatic "rescue": "I don't think it happened quite like that."

I heard the Red Cross say that casualties in Baghdad were so high, the hospitals had stopped counting.

I heard an old man say, after 11 members of his family—children and grandchildren—were killed when a tank blew up their minivan: "Our home is an empty place. We who are left are like wild animals. All we can do is cry out."

As the riots and looting broke out, I heard a man in the Baghdad market say: "Saddam Hussein's greatest crime is that he brought the American army to Iraq."

As the riots and looting broke out, I heard Donald Rumsfeld say: "It's untidy, and freedom's untidy."

I heard him say: "I picked up a newspaper today and I couldn't believe it. I read eight headlines that talked about chaos, violence, unrest. And it just was Henny Penny 'The sky is falling.' I've never seen anything like it! And here is a country that's being liberated, here are people who are going from being repressed and held under the thumb of a vicious dictator, and they're free. And all this newspaper could do, with eight or ten headlines, they showed a man bleeding, a civilian, who they claimed we had shot—one thing after another. It's just unbelievable."

And when the National Museum was emptied and the National Library burned down, I heard Donald Rumsfield say: "The images you are seeing on television you are seeing over, and over, and over, and it's the same picture of some person walking out of some building with a vase, and you see it 20 times, and you think, 'My goodness, were there that many vases? Is it possible that there were that many vases in the whole country?'"

I heard that 10,000 Iraqi civilians were dead.

◆ ◆ ◆

I heard Colin Powell say: "I'm absolutely sure that there are weapons of mass destruction there and the evidence will be forthcoming. We're just getting it now."

I heard the President say: "We'll find them. It'll be a matter of time to do so."

I heard Donald Rumsfeld say: "We know where they are. They're in the area around Tikrit and Baghdad, and east, west, south, and north, somewhat."

I heard the US was building fourteen "enduring bases," capable of housing 110,000 soldiers, and I heard Brigadier General Mark Kimmitt call them "a blueprint for how we could operate in the Middle East." I heard that the US was building its largest embassy in the world.

I heard that it would be a matter of months until Starbuck's and McDonald's opened branches in Baghdad. I heard that the HSBC bank would have cash machines all over the country.

I heard about the trade fairs run by New Bridges Strategies, a consulting firm that promised access to the Iraqi market. I heard one of its partners say: "Getting the rights to distribute Proctor & Gamble can be a gold mine. One well-stocked 7-Eleven could knock out thirty Iraqi stores. A Wal-Mart could take over the country."

On May 1, 2003, I heard the President, dressed up as a pilot, under a banner that read "Mission Accomplished," declare that combat operations were over: "The battle of Iraq is one victory in a war on terror that began on September the 11th, 2001." I heard him say: "The liberation of Iraq is a crucial advance in the campaign against terror. We've removed an ally of al-Qaeda, and cut off a source of terrorist funding. And this much is certain: No terrorist network will gain weapons of mass destruction from the Iraqi regime, because the regime is no more. In these 19 months that changed the world, our actions have been focused and deliberate and proportionate to the offense. We have not forgotten the victims of September the 11th—the last phone calls, the cold murder of children, the searches in the rubble. With those attacks, the terrorists and their supporters declared war on the United States. And war is what they got."

On May 1, 2003, I heard that 140 American soldiers had died in combat in Iraq.

I heard Richard Perle tell Americans to "relax and celebrate victory." I heard him say: "The predictions of those who opposed this war can be discarded like spent cartridges."

I heard Lieutenant General Jay Garner say: "We ought to look in a mirror and get proud and stick out our chests and suck in our bellies and say: 'Damn, we're Americans.'"

And later I heard that I could buy a 12-inch "Elite Force Aviator: George W. Bush" action figure: "Exacting in detail and fully equipped with authentic gear, this limited-edition action figure is a meticulous 1:6 scale recreation of the Commander-in-Chief's appearance during his historic Aircraft Carrier landing. This fully poseable figure features a realistic head sculpt, fully detailed cloth flight suit, helmet with oxygen mask, survival vest, g-pants, parachute harness and much more."

In February 2003, a month before the invasion, I heard General Eric Shinseki tell Congress that "several hundred thousand troops" would be needed to occupy Iraq. I heard him ridiculed by Paul Wolfowitz as "wildly off the mark." I heard that the Secretary of the Army, Thomas White, a former General, was fired for agreeing with Shinseki. In May 2003, I heard that Pentagon planners had predicted that US troop levels would fall to 30,000 by the end of the summer.

◆ ◆ ◆

I heard that Paul Bremer's first act as Director of the Coalition Provisional Authority was to fire all senior members of the Baath Party, including 100,000 civil servants, policemen, teachers, and doctors, and to dismiss all 400,000 soldiers of the Iraqi Army without pay or pensions. Two million people were dependent on that income. Since America supports private gun ownership, the soldiers were allowed to keep their weapons.

I heard that hundreds were being kidnapped and raped in Baghdad alone; that schools, hospitals, shops, and factories were being looted; that it was impossible to restore the electricity because all the copper wire had been stolen from the power plants.

I heard Paul Bremer say: "Most of the country is, in fact, orderly," and that all the problems were coming from "several hundred hard-core terrorists" from al-Qaeda and affiliated groups.

As attacks on American troops increased, I heard the generals disagree about who was fighting: Islamic fundamentalists or remnants of the Baath Party or Iraqi mercenaries or foreign mercenaries or ordinary citizens taking revenge for the loss of loved ones. I heard the President and the Vice President and the politicians and the television reporters simply call them "terrorists."

I heard the President say: "There are some who feel like that conditions are such that they can attack us there. My answer is: Bring them on! We have the force necessary to deal with the situation."

I heard that 25,000 Iraqi civilians were dead.

I heard Arnold Schwarzenegger, then campaigning for Governor and in Baghdad for a special showing to the troops of *Terminator 3*, say: "It is really wild driving round here, I mean the poverty, and you see there is no money, it is disastrous financially and there is the leadership vacuum, pretty much like California."

I heard that the Army was wrapping entire villages in barbed wire, with signs that read: "This fence is here for your protection. Do not approach or try to cross, or you will be shot." In one of those villages, I heard a man named Tariq say: "I see no difference between us and the Palestinians."

I heard Captain Todd Brown say: "You have to understand the Arab mind. The only thing they understand is force—force, pride, and saving face."

I heard that the US, as "a gift from the American people to the Iraqi people," had committed $18.4 billion to the reconstruction of basic infrastructure, but that future Iraqi governments would have no say in how the money was spent. I heard that the economy had been opened to foreign ownership, and that this could not be changed. I heard that the Iraqi army would be under the command of the US, and that this could not be changed. I heard, however, that "full authority" for health and hospitals had been turned over to the Iraqis, and that senior American health advisers had been withdrawn. I heard Tommy Thompson, Secretary of Health and Human Services, say that Iraq's hospitals would be fine if the Iraqis "just washed their hands and cleaned the crap off the walls."

I heard Colonel Nathan Sassaman say: "With a heavy dose of fear and violence, and a lot of money for projects, I think we can convince these people that we are here to help them."

I heard Richard Perle say: "Next year at about this time, I expect there will be a really thriving trade in the region, and we will see rapid economic development. And a year from now, I'll be very surprised if there is not some grand square in Baghdad named after President Bush."

◆ ◆ ◆

I heard about Operation Ivy Cyclone. I heard about Operation Vigilant Resolve. I heard about Operation Plymouth Rock. I heard about Operation Iron Hammer, its name taken from *Eisenhammer*, the Nazi plan to destroy Soviet generating plants.

I heard that Air Force regulations require that any airstrike likely to result in the deaths of more than thirty civilians must be personally approved by the Secretary of Defense, and I heard that Donald Rumsfeld approved every proposal.

I heard a Marine colonel say: "We napalmed those bridges. Unfortunately, there were people there. It's no great way to die."

I heard a Marine describe "dead-checking": "They teach us to do dead-checking when we're clearing rooms. You put two bullets into the guy's chest and one in the brain. But when you enter a room where guys are wounded, you might not know if they're alive or dead. So they teach us to dead-check them by pressing them in the eye with your boot, because generally a person, even if he's faking being dead, will flinch if you poke him there. If he moves, you put a bullet in the brain. You do this to keep the momentum going when you're flowing through a building. You don't want a guy popping up behind you and shooting you."

I heard the President say: "We're rolling back the terrorist threat, not on the fringes of its influence but at the heart of its power."

When the death toll of American soldiers reached 500, I heard Brigadier General Kimmitt say: "I don't think the soldiers are looking at arbitrary figures such as casualty counts as the barometer of their morale. They know they have a nation that stands behind them."

I heard an American soldier, standing next to his Humvee, say: "We liberated Iraq. Now the people here don't want us here, and guess what? We don't want to be here either. So why are we still here? Why don't they bring us home?"

I heard Colin Powell say: "We did not expect it would be quite this intense this long."

I heard Donald Rumsfeld say: "We're facing a test of will."

I heard the President say: "We found biological laboratories. They're illegal. They're against the United Nations resolutions, and we've so far discovered two. And we'll find more weapons as time goes on. But for those who say we haven't found the banned manufacturing devices or banned weapons, they're wrong, we found them."

I heard Tony Blair say: "The remains of 400,000 human beings have been found in mass graves." And I saw his words repeated in a US government pamphlet, *Iraq's Legacy of Terror: Mass Graves*, and on a US government website, which said this represents "a crime against humanity surpassed only by the Rwandan genocide of 1994, Pol Pot's Cambodian killing fields in the 1970s, and the Nazi Holocaust of World War II."

◆ ◆ ◆

I heard the President say: "Today, on bended knee, I thank the good Lord for protecting those of our troops overseas, and our coalition troops and innocent Iraqis who suffer at the hands of some of these senseless killings by people who are trying to shake our will."

I heard that this was the first American President in wartime who had never attended a funeral for a dead soldier. I heard that photographs of the flag-draped coffins returning home were banned. I heard that the Pentagon had renamed "body bags" as "transfer tubes."

I heard a tearful George Bush Sr., speaking at the annual convention of the National Petrochemical and Refiners Association, say that it was "deeply offensive and contemptible" the way "elites and intellectuals" were dismissing "the sowing of the seeds of basic freedom in that troubled part of the world." I heard him say: "It hurts an awful lot more when it's your son that is being criticized."

I heard the President's mother say: "Why should we hear about body bags, and deaths? Why should I waste my beautiful mind on something like that?"

I heard that 7% of all American military deaths in Iraq were suicides, that 10% of the soldiers evacuated to the Army hospital in Landstuhl, Germany, had been sent for "psychiatric or behavioral health issues," and that 20% of the military was expected to suffer from post-traumatic stress disorder.

I heard Brigadier General Kimmitt deny that civilians were being killed: "We run extremely precise operations."

I heard Donald Rumsfeld say that the fighting was just the work of "thugs, gangs, and terrorists." I heard General Richard Myers say: "It's not a Shi'ite uprising. Moktada al-Sadr has a very small following." I heard that an unnamed "intelligence official" said: "Hatred of the American occupation has spread rapidly among Shi'i, and is now so large that Mr. Sadr and his forces represent just one element. Destroying his Mahdi Army might be possible only by destroying Sadr City." Sadr City is the most populated part of Baghdad. I heard that, among the Sunnis, former Baath Party leaders and Saddam loyalists had been joined by Sunni tribal chiefs.

I heard that there were now thirty separate militias in the country. I heard the television news reporters routinely refer to them as "anti-Iraqi forces."

I heard that Paul Bremer closed down a popular newspaper, *Al-Hawza*, because of "inaccurate reporting."

As Shias in Sadr City lined up to donate blood for Sunnis in Fallujah, I heard a man say: "We should thank Paul Bremer. He has finally united Iraq—against him."

I heard the President say: "I wouldn't be happy if I were occupied either."

◆ ◆ ◆

I heard Tony Blair say: "Before people crow about the absence of weapons of mass destruction, I suggest they wait a bit."

I heard General Myers say: "Given time, given the number of prisoners now that we're interrogating, I'm confident that we're going to find weapons of mass destruction."

I heard the President say: "Prisoners are being taken, and intelligence is being gathered. Our decisive actions will continue until these enemies of democracy are dealt with."

I heard a soldier describe what they called "bitch in a box": "That was the normal procedure for them when they wanted to soften up a prisoner: stuff them in the trunk for a while and drive them around. The hoods I can understand, and to have them cuffed with the plastic things—that I could see. But the trunk episode—I thought it was kind of unusual. It was like a sweatbox, let's face it. In Iraq, in August, it's hitting 120 degrees, and you can imagine what it was like in a trunk of a black Mercedes."

I heard a National Guardsman from Florida say: "We had a sledgehammer that we would bang against the wall, and that would create an echo that sounds like an explosion that scared the hell out of them. If that didn't work we would load a 9mm pistol, and pretend to be charging it near their head, and make them think we were going to shoot them. Once you did that, they did whatever you wanted them to do basically. The way we treated these men was hard even for the soldiers, especially after realizing that many of these 'combatants' were no more than shepherds."

I heard a Marine at Camp Whitehorse say: "The 50/10 technique was used to break down EPWs and make it easier for the HET member to get information from them." The 50/10 technique was to make prisoners stand for fifty minutes of the hour for ten hours with a hood over their heads in the heat. EPWs were "enemy prisoners of war." HETs were "human exploitation teams."

I heard Captain Donald Reese, a prison warden, say: "It was not uncommon to see people without clothing. I was told the 'whole nudity thing' was an interrogation procedure used by military intelligence, and never thought much about it."

I heard Donald Rumsfeld say: "I have not seen anything thus far that says that the people abused were abused in the process of interrogating them or for interrogation purposes."

I heard Private Lynndie England, who was photographed in Abu Ghraib holding a prisoner on a leash: "I was instructed by persons in higher rank to stand there, hold this leash, look at the camera, and they took pictures for PsyOps [Psychological Operations]. I didn't really, I mean, want to be in any picture. I thought it was kind of weird."

Detainees 27, 30, and 31 were stripped of their clothing, handcuffed together nude, placed on the ground, and forced to lie on each other and simulate sex while photographs were taken. Detainee 8 had his food thrown in the toilet and was then ordered to eat it. Detainee 7 was ordered to bark like a dog while MPs spat and urinated on him; he was sodomized with a police stick as two female MPs watched. Detainee 3 was sodomized with a broom by a female soldier. Detainee 15 was photographed standing on a box with a hood on his head and simulated electrical wires attached to his hands and penis. Detainees 1, 16, 17, 18, 23, 24, and 26 were placed in a pile and forced to masturbate while photographs were taken. An unidentified detainee was photographed covered in feces with a banana inserted in his anus. Detainee 5 watched Civilian 1 rape an unidentified 15-year-old male detainee while a female soldier took photographs. Detainees 5 and 7 were stripped of their clothing and forced to wear women's underwear on their heads. Detainee 28, handcuffed with his hands behind his back in a shower stall, was declared dead when an MP removed the sandbag from his head and checked his pulse.

I heard Donald Rumsfeld say: "If you are in Washington, D.C., you can't know what's going on in the midnight shift in one of those many prisons around the world."

◆ ◆ ◆

I heard that the Red Cross had to close its offices because it was too dangerous. I heard that General Electric and the Siemens Corporation had to close their offices. I heard that Doctors Without Borders had to leave, and that journalists rarely left their hotels. I heard that, after their headquarters was bombed, most of the United Nations staff had gone. I heard that the cost of life insurance policies for the few remaining Western businessmen was $10,000 a week.

I heard Tom Foley, Director of Iraq Private-Sector Development, say: "The security risks are not as bad as they appear on TV. Western civilians are not the targets themselves. These are acceptable risks."

I heard the spokesman for Paul Bremer say: "We have isolated pockets where we are encountering problems."

I heard that, no longer able to rely on the military for help, private security firms had banded together to form the largest private army in the world, with its own rescue teams and intelligence. I heard that there were some 20,000 mercenary soldiers, now called "private contractors," in Iraq, earning as much as $2,000 a day, and not subject to Iraqi or US military law.

I heard that 50,000 Iraqi civilians were dead.

I heard that, on a day when a car bomb killed three Americans, Paul Bremer's last act as Director of the Coalition Provisional Authority was to issue laws making it illegal to drive with only one hand on the steering wheel or to honk a horn when there is no emergency.

I heard that the unemployment rate was now 70%, that less than 1% of the work force was engaged in reconstruction, and that the US had spent only 2% of the $18.4 billion approved by Congress for reconstruction. I heard that an official audit could not account for $8.8 billion of Iraqi oil money given to Iraqi ministries by the Coalition Provisional Authority.

I heard the President say: "Our Coalition is standing with

responsible Iraqi leaders as they establish growing authority in their country."

I heard that, a few days before he became Prime Minister, Ayad Allawi visited a Baghdad police station where six suspected insurgents, blindfolded and handcuffed, were lined up against a wall. I heard that, as four Americans and a dozen Iraqi policemen watched, Allawi pulled out a pistol and shot each prisoner in the head. I heard that he said that this is how we must deal with insurgents. I heard that this story was not true, and then I heard that even if it weren't true, it was believable.

On June 28, 2004, with the establishment of an interim government, I heard the Vice President say: "After decades of rule by a brutal dictator, Iraq has been returned to its rightful owners, the people of Iraq."

This was the military summary for an ordinary day, July 22, 2004, a day that produced no headlines: "Two roadside bombs exploded next to a van and a Mercedes in separate areas of Baghdad, killing four civilians. A gunman in a Toyota opened fire on a police checkpoint and escaped. Police wounded three gunmen at a checkpoint and arrested four men suspected of attempted murder. Seven more roadside bombs exploded in Baghdad and gunmen twice attacked US troops. Police dismantled a car bomb in Mosul and gunmen attacked the Western driver of a gravel truck at Tell Afar. There were three roadside bombings and a rocket attack on US troops in Mosul and another gun attack on US forces near Tell Afar. At Taji, a civilian vehicle collided with a US military vehicle, killing six civilians and injuring seven others. At Bayji, a US vehicle hit a landmine. Gunmen murdered a dentist at the Ad Dwar hospital. There were 17 roadside bomb explosions against US forces in Taji, Baquba, Baqua, Jalula, Tikrit, Paliwoda, Balad, Samarra and Duluiyeh, with attacks by gunmen on US troops in Tikrit and Balad. A headless body in an orange jump-suit was found in the Tigris; believed to be Bulgarian hostage, Ivalyo Kepov. Kirkuk air base attacked. Five roadside bombs on US forces in Rutbah, Kalso and Ramadi. Gunmen attacked Americans in Fallujah and Ramadi. The police chief of Najaf was abducted. Two civilian contractors were attacked by gunmen at Haswah. A roadside bomb exploded near Kerbala and Hillah. International forces were attacked by gunmen at Al Qurnah."

◆ ◆ ◆

I heard the President say: "You can embolden an enemy by sending a mixed message. You can dispirit the Iraqi people by sending mixed messages. That's why I will continue to lead with clarity and in a resolute way."

I heard the President say: "Today, because the world acted with courage and moral clarity, Iraqi athletes are competing in the Olympic Games." Iraq had sent teams to the previous Olympics. And when the President ran a campaign advertisement with the flags of Iraq and Afghanistan and the words "At this Olympics there will be two more free nations—and two fewer terrorist regimes," I heard the Iraqi coach say: "Iraq as a team does not want Mr. Bush to use us for the presidential campaign. He can find another way to advertise himself." I heard their star midfielder say that if he weren't playing soccer he'd be fighting for the resistance in Fallujah: "Bush has committed so many crimes. How will he meet his god having slaughtered so many men and women?"

I heard an unnamed "senior British Army officer" invoke the Nazis to describe what he saw: "My view and the view of the British chain of command is that the Americans' use of violence is not proportionate and is over-responsive to the threat they are facing. They don't see the Iraqi people the way we see them. They view them as *Untermenschen* [subhumans]. They are not concerned about the Iraqi loss of life. As far as they are concerned Iraq is bandit country and everybody is out to kill them. It is trite, but American troops do shoot first and ask questions later."

I heard Makki al-Nazzal, who was managing a clinic in Fallujah, say, in unaccented English: "I have been a fool for forty-seven years. I used to believe in European and American civilization."

I heard Donald Rumsfeld say: "We never believed that we'd just tumble over weapons of mass destruction."

I heard Condoleezza Rice say: "We never expected we were going to open garages and find them."

I heard Donald Rumsfeld say: "They may have had time to destroy them, and I don't know the answer."

I heard Richard Perle say: "We don't know where to look for them and we never did know where to look for them. I hope this will take less than 200 years."

◆ ◆ ◆

I heard the President say: "I know what I'm doing when it comes to winning this war."

I heard the President say: "I'm a war president."

I heard that 1,000 American soldiers were dead and 7,000 wounded in combat. I heard that there was now an average of 87 attacks a day on US troops.

I heard Condoleezza Rice say: "Not everything has gone as we would have liked it to."

I heard Colin Powell say: "We did miscalculate the difficulty."

I heard an unnamed "senior US diplomat in Baghdad" say: "We're dealing with a population that hovers between bare tolerance and outright hostility. This idea of a functioning democracy is crazy. We thought there would be a reprieve after sovereignty, but all hell is breaking loose."

I heard Major Thomas Neemeyer say: "The only way to stomp out the insurgency of the mind would be to kill the entire population."

I heard the CNN reporter near the Tomb of Ali in Najaf, a city that once had 500,000 people, say: "Everything outside of the mosque seems to be totaled."

I heard Khudeir Salman, who sold ice from a donkey cart in Najaf, say he was giving up after Marine snipers killed his friend, another ice-seller: "I found him this morning. The sniper shot his donkey too. And even the ambulance drivers are too scared to get the body."

I heard the Vice President say: "Such an enemy cannot be deterred, cannot be contained, cannot be appeased, or negotiated with. It can only be destroyed. And that is the business at hand."

I heard an unnamed "senior American commander" say: "We need to make a decision on when the cancer of Fallujah will be cut out."

I heard Major General John Batiste, outside of Samarra, say: "It'll be a quick fight and the enemy is going to die fast. The message for the people of Samarra is: Peacefully or not, this is going to be solved."

I heard Brigadier General Kimmitt say: "Our patience is not eternal."

I heard the President say: "America will never be run out of Iraq by a bunch of thugs and killers."

I heard about the wedding party that was attacked by American planes, killing 45 people, and the wedding photographer who videotaped the festivities until he himself was killed. And though the tape was shown on television, I heard Brigadier General Kimmet say: "There was no evidence of a wedding. There may have been some kind of celebration. Bad people have celebrations, too."

I heard an Iraqi man say: "I swear I saw dogs eating the body of a woman."

I heard an Iraqi man say: "We have at least 700 dead. So many of them are children and women. The stench from the dead bodies in parts of the city is unbearable."

I heard Donald Rumsfeld say: "Death has a tendency to encourage a depressing view of war."

◆ ◆ ◆

On the occasion of Ayad Allawi's visit to the United States, I heard the President say: "What's important for the American people to hear is reality. And the reality is right here in the form of the Prime Minister."

Asked about ethnic tensions, I heard Ayad Allawi say: "There are no problems between Shia and Sunnis and Kurds and Arabs and Turkmen. Usually we have no problems of ethnic or religious nature in Iraq."

I heard him say: "There is nothing, no problem, except on a small pocket in Fallujah."

I heard Colonel Jerry Durant say, after a meeting with Ramadi tribal sheiks: "A lot of these guys have read history, and they said to me the government in Baghdad is like the Vichy government in France during World War II."

I heard a journalist say: "I am house-bound. I leave when I have a very good reason to and a scheduled interview. I avoid going to people's homes and never walk in the streets. I can't go grocery shopping any more, can't eat in restaurants, can't strike up a conversation with strangers, can't look for stories, can't drive in anything but a full armored car, can't go to scenes of breaking news stories, can't be stuck in traffic, can't speak English outside, can't take a road trip, can't say I'm an American, can't linger at checkpoints, can't be curious about what people are saying, doing, feeling."

I heard Donald Rumsfeld say: "It's a tough part of the world. We had something like 200 or 300 or 400 people killed in many of the major cities of America last year. What's the difference? We just didn't see each homicide in every major city in the United States on television every night."

I heard that 80,000 Iraqi civilians were dead. I heard that the war had already cost $225 billion and was continuing at the rate of $40 billion a month. I heard there was now an average of 130 attacks a day on US troops.

I heard Captain John Mountford say: "I just wonder what would have happened if we had worked a little more with the locals."

I heard that, in the last year alone, the US had fired 127 tons of Depleted Uranium (DU) munitions in Iraq, the atomicity equivalent of approximately 10,000 Nagasaki bombs. I heard that the widespread use of DU in the first Gulf War was believed to be the primary cause of the health problems suffered among its 580,400 veterans. 467 were wounded in the war. Ten years later, 11,000 were dead, and 325,000 on medical disability. DU carried in semen led to high rates of endometriosis, often leading to hysterectomies, in their wives and girlfriends. Of soldiers who had healthy babies before the war, 67% of their post-war babies were born with severe defects, including missing legs, arms, organs, or eyes.

I heard that 380 tons of HMX (High Melting Point Explosive) and RDX (Rapid Detonation Explosive) were missing from al-Qaqaa, one of Iraq's "most sensitive military installations," which had never been guarded after the invasion. I heard that one pound of these explosives was enough to blow up a 747 jet, and that this cache could be used to make a million roadside bombs, which were the cause of half the casualties among US troops.

I heard Donald Rumsfeld say, when asked why the troops were being kept in the war much longer than their normal tours of duty: "Oh, come on. People are fungible. You can have them here or there." "Fungible" means "interchangeable."

◆ ◆ ◆

I heard Colonel Gary Brandl say: "The enemy has got a face. He's called Satan. He's in Fallujah and we're going to destroy him."

I heard a Marine commander tell his men: "You will be held accountable for the facts not as they are in hindsight but as they appeared to you at the time. If, in your mind, you fire to protect yourself or your men, you are doing the right thing. It doesn't matter if later on we find out you wiped out a family of unarmed civilians."

I heard Lieutenant Colonel Mark Smith say: "We're going out where the bad guys live, and we're going to slay them in their ZIP code."

I heard that 15,000 US troops invaded Fallujah, as planes dropped 500-pound bombs on "insurgent targets." I heard they destroyed the Nazzal Emergency Hospital in the center of the city, killing 20 doctors. I heard they occupied Fallujah General Hospital, which the military had called a "center of propaganda" for reporting civilian casualties. I heard that they confiscated all mobile phones and refused to allow doctors and ambulances to go out and help the wounded. I heard they bombed the power plant to black out the city, and that the water was shut off. I heard that every house and shop had a large red X spray-painted on the door to indicate that it had been searched.

I heard Donald Rumsfeld say: "Innocent civilians in that city have all the guidance they need as to how they can avoid getting into trouble. There aren't going to be large numbers of civilians killed and certainly not by US forces."

I heard that, in a city of 150 mosques, there were no longer any calls to prayer.

I heard Muhammad Aboud tell how, unable to leave his house to go to a hospital, he had watched his nine-year-old son bleed to death, and how, unable to leave his house to go to a cemetery, he had buried his son in the garden.

I heard Sami al-Jumali, a doctor, say: "There is not a single surgeon in Fallujah. A 13-year-old child just died in my hands."

I heard an American soldier say: "We will win the hearts and minds of Fallujah by ridding the city of insurgents. We're doing that by patrolling the streets and killing the enemy."

I heard an American soldier, a Bradley gunner, say: "I was basically looking for any clean walls, you know, without any holes in them. And then we were putting holes in them."

I heard Farhan Saleh say: "My kids are hysterical with fear. They are traumatized by the sound but there is nowhere to take them."

I heard that the US troops allowed women and children to leave the city, but that all "military-age males," men from 15 to 60, were required to stay. I heard that no food or medicine was allowed into the city.

I heard the Red Cross say that at least 800 civilians had died. I heard Ayad Allawi say there were no civilian casualties in Fallujah.

I heard a man named Abu Sabah say: "They used these weird bombs that put up smoke like a mushroom cloud. Then small pieces fall from the air with long tails of smoke behind them." I heard him say that pieces of these bombs exploded into large fires that burnt the skin even when water was thrown on it. I heard him say: "People suffered so much from these."

I heard Kassem Muhammad Ahmed say: "I watched them roll

over wounded people in the streets with tanks. This happened so many times."

I heard a man named Khalil say: "They shot women and old men in the streets. Then they shot anyone who tried to get their bodies."

I heard Nihida Kadhim, a housewife, say that when she was finally allowed to return to her home, she found a message written with lipstick on her living-room mirror: "FUCK IRAQ AND EVERY IRAQI IN IT."

I heard General John Sattler say that the destruction of Fallujah had "broken the back of the insurgency."

I heard that three fourths of Fallujah had been shelled into rubble. I heard an American soldier say: "It's kind of bad we destroyed everything, but at least we gave them a chance for a new start."

I heard that only five roads into Fallujah would remain open. The rest would be sealed with "sand berms," mountains of earth. At the entry points, everyone would be photographed, fingerprinted, and have iris scans taken before being issued identification cards. All citizens would be required to wear identification cards in plain sight at all times. No private automobiles—the vehicle of suicide bombings—would be allowed in the city. All males would be organized into "work brigades" rebuilding the city. They would be paid, but participation would be compulsory.

I heard Muhammad Kubaissy, a shopkeeper, say: "I am still searching for what they have been calling democracy."

I heard a soldier say that he had talked to his priest about killing Iraqis, and that his priest had told him it was all right to kill for his government as long as he did not enjoy it. After he had killed at least four men, I heard the soldier say that he had begun to have doubts: "Where the fuck did Jesus say it's OK to kill people for your government?"

◆ ◆ ◆

I heard Donald Rumsfeld say: "I don't believe anyone that I know in the administration ever said that Iraq had nuclear weapons."

I heard Donald Rumsfeld say: "The coalition did not act in Iraq because we had discovered dramatic new evidence of Iraq's pursuit of weapons of mass murder. We acted because we saw the evidence in a dramatic new light, through the prism of our experience on 9/11."

I heard a reporter say to Donald Rumsfeld, "Before the war in Iraq, you stated the case very eloquently and you said they would welcome us with open arms." And I heard Rumsfeld interrupt him: "Never said that. Never did. You may remember it well, but you're thinking of somebody else. You can't find, anywhere, me saying anything like those things you just said I said."

I heard Ahmad Chalabi, who had supplied most of the information about the weapons of mass destruction, shrug and say: "We are heroes in error. . . . What was said before is not important."

I heard Paul Wolfowitz say: "For bureaucratic reasons, we settled on one issue, weapons of mass destruction, as justification for invading Iraq, because it was the one reason everyone could agree on."

I heard Condoleezza Rice continue to insist: "It's not as if anybody believes that Saddam Hussein was without weapons of mass destruction."

I heard that the Niger "yellowcake" uranium was a hoax, that the aluminum tubes could not be used for nuclear weapons, that the mobile biological laboratories produced helium for weather balloons, that the fleet of unmanned aerial "drones" was a single broken-down oversized model airplane, that Saddam had no elaborate underground bunkers, that Colin Powell's primary source, his "solid intelligence," for the evidence he presented at the United Nations was a paper, written ten years before, by a graduate student. I heard that, of the 400,000 bodies buried in mass graves, only 5,000 had been found.

I heard Lieutenant General James Conway say: "It was a surprise to me then, and it remains a surprise to me now, that we have not uncovered weapons. It's not from lack of trying."

I heard a reporter ask Donald Rumsfeld: "If Iraq did not have WMDs, why did they pose an immediate threat to this country?" I heard Rumsfeld answer: "You and a few other critics are the only people I've heard use the phrase 'immediate threat.' It's become a kind of folklore that that's what happened. If you have any citations, I'd like to see them." And I heard the reporter read: "No terrorist state poses a greater or immediate threat to the security of our people." Rumsfeld replied: "It—my view of—of the situation was that he—he had—we—we believe, the best intelligence that we had and other countries had and that—that we believed and we still do not know—we will know."

I heard Sa'adoon al-Zubaydi, an interpreter who lived in the Presidential palace, say: "For at least three years Saddam

Hussein had been tired of the day-to-day management of his regime. He could not stand it any more: meetings, commissions, dispatches, telephone calls. So he withdrew. . . Alone, isolated, out of it. He preferred shutting himself up in his office, writing novels."

◆ ◆ ◆

I heard the President say that Iraq is a "catastrophic success."

I heard Donald Rumsfeld say: "They haven't won a single battle the entire time since the end of major combat operations."

I heard that hundreds of schools had been completely destroyed and thousands looted, and that most people thought it too dangerous to send their children to school. I heard there was no system of banks. I heard that, in the cities, there were only 10 hours of electricity a day and only 60% of the people had drinkable water. I heard that the malnutrition of children was now far worse than in Uganda or Haiti. I heard that none of the 270,000 babies born after the start of the war had received immunizations.

I heard General Muhammad Abdullah Shahwani, the chief of Iraqi intelligence, say that there were now 200,000 active fighters in the insurgency.

I heard Donald Rumsfeld say: "I don't believe it's our job to reconstruct that country. The Iraqi people are going to have to reconstruct that country over a period of time." I heard him say that, in any event, "the infrastructure of that country was not terribly damaged by the war at all."

I heard that the American Ambassador, John Negroponte, had requested that $3.37 billion intended for water, sewage, and electricity projects be transferred to security and oil output.

I heard that the reporters from the al-Jazeera network were indefinitely banned. I heard Donald Rumsfeld say: "What al-Jazeera is doing is vicious, inaccurate, and inexcusable."

I heard that Spain left the Coalition of the Willing. Hungary left; the Dominican Republic left; Nicaragua left; Honduras left. I heard that the Philippines had left early, after a Filipino truckdriver was kidnapped and executed. Norway left. Portugal, Singapore, and Tonga left. Poland, Ukraine, and the Netherlands said they were leaving. Thailand said it was leaving. Bulgaria was reducing its few hundred troops. Moldova first cut its force from 42 to 12, and then left.

I heard that the President had once said: "Two years from now, only the Brits may be with us. At some point, we may be the only ones left. That's OK with me. We are America."

I heard a reporter ask Lieutenant General Jay Garner how long the troops would remain in Iraq, and I heard him reply: "I hope they're there for a long time."

I heard General Tommy Franks say: "One has to think about the numbers. I think we will be engaged with our military in Iraq for perhaps three, five, perhaps ten years."

I heard that the Pentagon was now exploring what it called the "Salvador option," modeled on the death squads in El Salvador in the 1980s, when John Negroponte was Ambassador to Honduras and when Elliot Abrams, now White House Adviser on the Middle East, called the massacre at El Mozote "nothing but Communist propaganda." Under the plan, the US would advise, train, and support paramilitaries in assassination and kidnapping, including secret raids across the Syrian border. In the Vice Presidential debate, I heard the Vice President say: "Twenty years ago we had a similar situation in El Salvador. We had a guerrilla insurgency that controlled roughly a third of the country. . . And today El Salvador is a whale of a lot better."

I heard that 100,000 Iraqi civilians were dead. I heard that there was now an average of 150 attacks a day on US troops. I heard that, in Baghdad, 700 people were being killed every month in "non-war-related" criminal activities. I heard that 1,400 American soldiers had been killed and that the true casualty figure was approximately 25,000.

I heard that Donald Rumsfeld had a machine sign his letters of condolence to the families of soldiers who had been killed. When this caused a small scandal, I heard him say: "I have directed that in the future I sign each letter."

I heard the President say: "The credibility of the United States is based upon our strong desire to make the world more peaceful, and the world is now more peaceful."

I heard the President say: "I want to be the peace President. The next four years will be peaceful years."

I heard Attorney General John Ashcroft say, on the day of his resignation: "The objective of securing the safety of Americans from crime and terror has been achieved."

I heard the President say: "For a while we were marching to war. Now we're marching to peace."

I heard that the US military had purchased 1,500,000,000 bullets for use in the coming year. That is 58 bullets for every Iraqi adult and child.

I heard that Saddam Hussein, in solitary confinement, was spending his time writing poetry, reading the Qu'ran, eating cookies and muffins, and taking care of some bushes and shrubs. I heard that he had placed a circle of white stones around a small plum tree.

ACKNOWLEDGMENTS

These essays were written for publication abroad. If nothing else, they helped to demonstrate that the US was not a monolith of opinion, as was commonly believed in much of the world until the 2004 Presidential election.

In English, the articles tended to circulate via e-mail among individuals, turning up on blogs, websites, chat groups, and listservs. For writing of this kind, it is a happy way to publish: the readers vote with their forward buttons.

I am a literary writer, not an expert, an insider, a professional pundit. The "chronicle" essays are snapshots of what one person who reads the newspapers was thinking on certain given days in recent history. I was inspired by the writings of Don McNeill, who drowned in 1968 at age 23, and who used to send weekly reports on the zeitgeist to the *Village Voice* and other alternative New York newspapers.

Some of what I wrote has been overtaken by events or new information. In some cases, time has shifted emphases. I have, however, resisted the temptation to change or delete or add anything to the original articles, other than the partial elimination of the repetitions that occur when discrete pieces are gathered together. The writing is intended to remain attached to the day on which it was written; the facts (for example, the casualty figures for September 11) are what were known or thought that day.

"Republicans" and "What I Heard About Iraq" were inspired by Charles Reznikoff, who sifted through countless volumes of court records to produce his booklength poems, *Testimony* and *Holocaust*. The research for both essays was largely dependent on an archive I had amassed thanks to the extraordinary, unpaid labors of the poet Geoffrey Gardner, whose one-man Anarkiss Newswire has been collecting and e-mailing thousands of articles from the world press once or twice a day, nearly every day of the Bush years.

Portions of this book were first published as a pamphlet, *9/12*, by Prickly Paradigm Press. (My thanks to Marshall Sahlins and Matthew Engelke.) A Spanish translation by Aurelio Major was published in Spain by Ediciones Bronce and in Mexico by Era. (Thanks to Valerie Miles and Marcelo Uribe.) "The City of Peace" is reprinted from my book *Outside Stories* (New Directions, 1992).

The essays were particularly encouraged by Frank Berberich of *Lettre International*, Germany, which published many of them. Others appeared in *Byron Bay Echo* and *Masthead* in Australia; *Alligator, Yang,* and *Streven* in (Flemish) Belgium; *Fantom Slobode* in Bosnia; *Dialogos & Debates de Escola Paulista de Magistratura* in Brazil; *Tianya* in China; *El Malpensante* in Colombia; *The Feral Tribune* in Croatia; *Granma* in Cuba; *Zvedavec* in the Czech Republic; *Lettre Internationale, Faklen,* and *Information* in Denmark; *D'Autres Espaces, L'Hebdoryphore,* and *La Revue des Resources* in France; *Magyar Lettre International* in Hungary; *Outlook, The Hindu,* and *The Kashmir Times* in India; *Lettera Internazionale* in Italy; *Mambogani: The Voice of the Wananchi* in Kenya; *Confabulario, La Jornada, El Financiero, Reforma, Memoria,* and *Letras Libres* in Mexico; *Gazeta* in Poland; the al-Jazeera web-site in Qatar; *Peterburg na Nevskom* and *Krasny* in Russia; *Letra Internacional, La Vanguardia, Letras Libres,* and *Lateral* in Spain; *Ordfront* in Sweden; *Guney* in Turkey; and *Tien Phong* and *Van Nghe Tre* in Vietnam. In the US, a few were published or reprint-ed in *Tin House, Fellowship, CovertAction Quarterly,* and *The Brooklyn Rail*. "What I Heard About Iraq" was first published in the *London Review of Books* and reprinted as a book by Verso in the UK. I am grateful to the many translators and editors involved.